T0326288

THE COURAGE TO BE PRESENT

the courage to be present

BUDDHISM, PSYCHOTHERAPY,
AND THE AWAKENING OF
NATURAL WISDOM

Karen Kissel Wegela

SHAMBHALA
BOULDER
2010

Shambhala Publications, Inc.
2129 13th Street
Boulder, Colorado 80302
www.shambhala.com

Printed in the United States of America

Shambhala Publications makes every effort to print on acid-free, recycled
paper.

Shambhala Publications is distributed worldwide by Penguin Random
House, Inc., and its subsidiaries.

Designed by Gopa & Ted2, Inc.

The Library of Congress catalogues the hardcover edition
of this book as follows:
Wegela, Karen Kissel.
The courage to be present: Buddhism, psychotherapy, and the
awakening of natural wisdom / Karen Kissel Wegela.—1st ed.
p. cm.
Includes bibliographical references and index.
ISBN 978-1-59030-658-1 (hardcover: alk. paper)
ISBN 978-1-59030-830-1 (pbk.: alk. paper)
1. Psychotherapy—Religious aspects—Buddhism. 2. Buddhism—
Doctrines. 3. Meditation—Buddhism. 4. Paramitas (Buddhism) I. Title.
BQ4570.P76W44   2009
294.3'3615—dc22
2009003934

To Fred,
who gets me laughing when I lose all perspective

.

contents

acknowledgments

IN WRITING A BOOK that is grounded in the view of the interdependence of all beings and all phenomena, I became vividly aware of how indebted I am to countless people and circumstances. Still, there are some people I would especially like to acknowledge for their support, help, guidance, and teaching.

It has been my great good fortune to have been the student of many outstanding teachers, beginning with my incomparable root teacher, the Venerable Chögyam Trungpa Rinpoche. In addition, I have been privileged to learn from Khenchen Thrangu Rinpoche, Khenpo Tsültrim Gyamtso Rinpoche, Dzigar Kongtrul Rinpoche, Dzogchen Ponlop Rinpoche, Drubwang Tsoknyi Rinpoche, and Tenzin Gyatso, the Dalai Lama—all of the Tibetan Vajrayana tradition; from Thich Nhat Hanh of the Vietnamese Zen tradition; and also from Reb Zalman Schachter-Shalomi, who defies categorization. The Mahayana writings of both B. Alan Wallace and Pema Chödrön have also provided me with much-appreciated guidance. I would also like to mention Jonathan Eric, who probably never knew how deeply his kindness affected me at a meditation retreat in 1980.

I am grateful to my clients, who over the years have honored me with their trust and taught me so much about how to do useful psychotherapy. Without their generosity, I would have nothing to write about.

For the past twenty-eight years, my students at Naropa University have always asked exactly the right questions to reveal the gaps in my knowledge. They have insisted upon my continuing to clarify my understanding of the intersection of Buddhism and psychotherapy. Their own ideas about that integration have enriched my own, and they have also been kind enough to laugh at my jokes. For these things, and so much more, I thank them.

Jeremy Tharpa Lowry has been my main muse, beginning some years ago when he began lobbying me to write another book. He enlisted others in his campaign until I was beset on all sides by friendly encouragement to get started writing. I would like especially to express my appreciation to his main confederate, Jennie Hyatt. Jeremy has read the drafts of all the chapters as I have written them and has offered extremely useful suggestions for how to improve the text.

My colleagues at Naropa have been a source of tremendous inspiration, support, and humor. Our conversations about joining the principles of Buddhist thought with psychotherapy and with the training of psychotherapists have been provocative and delightful. I would like especially to thank Lauren Casalino, MacAndrew Jack, Robert Unger, Victoria Howard, and the late Edward Podvoll.

I would also like to acknowledge my indebtedness to Gay Watson, Maura Sills, Mark Epstein, and Harvey Aronson for their work and wisdom in bringing together the teachings of the Buddha and the practice of psychotherapy.

My peer consultant, the psychologist William Staudenmaier, has been an invaluable resource and support.

Emily Bower at Shambhala Publications has been astonishingly encouraging and heroically responsive to my many questions, anxieties, and confusions. I offer her my heartfelt gratitude.

I would like to thank my family, both living and no longer living, who cradled me with love, humor, and sharp minds: my parents, my sister Joie, my "brother" Lewey, my niece Debbie, and my many cousine, aunts, and uncles.

Finally, I would like to thank my husband, Fred, whose writer's eye, quirky mind, and generous heart have long nurtured both my writing and me.

introduction
what is a bodhisattva?

IN THE LATE 1970S, when I first started practicing and studying Buddhist meditation and philosophy, I learned of the ideal of the "bodhisattva," one who dedicates his or her life to the benefit of all other beings. I thought this notion was inspiring—inspiring, but crazy. A bodhisattva, I learned, was the Sanskrit word for one who put the needs and desires of all others before her own.

Put everyone before myself? I could hardly imagine letting someone go before me in the line at the supermarket. And anyway, isn't putting everyone else's needs first a psychological problem—one that we would come to call "codependency"? And yet, there was something that spoke to me, that touched my heart, in the ideal of the bodhisattva. I would have to look further.

I had already begun a regular "sitting practice" of meditation based on Buddhist teachings, which had become a source of immense relief to me at a particularly chaotic and difficult time in my life. Learning to simply be present, to touch my experience and also to let it go, had brought a sense of relaxation and aliveness to my mind and my life. I was grateful to have my meditation practice, and I suspected that the Buddhist teachings contained some essential sanity that I had not found elsewhere. So, I was curious about these bodhisattva teachings, even though they went against the grain of my habitual outlook. Up until now my meditation practice was clearly about me—me and my confusion, me and my pain, me and my relief. From the first moment

I heard of the bodhisattva ideal, I found it both attractive and a bit threatening.

My personal path has always included teaching, beginning in high school when my geometry teacher asked me to tutor a classmate. It has often been through teaching—and also writing—that I have clarified my own understanding. For more than twenty-five years I have been a core faculty member at Naropa University in Boulder, Colorado, where I have taught "contemplative psychotherapy"—a field of study that brings together Buddhist teachings and psychotherapy training—in one of its graduate psychology programs.

A few years ago I had to fill in for another teacher at the last minute. She was scheduled to teach a class on the *Bodhicharyavatara*[1] (Sanskrit for "The Bodhisattva's Way of Life"), a classic text by the eighth-century Buddhist scholar and meditation master Shantideva. In the contemplative psychotherapy program, we study this text for the light it sheds on how to integrate the teachings on the bodhisattva path and the contemporary practice of psychotherapy. I have continued to teach that class, among others, and it continues to give me the opportunity to explore the bodhisattva teachings, which I am then able to apply in my own psychotherapy practice.

The bodhisattva teachings are at the heart of the school of Buddhism known as the *Mahayana* (Sanskrit for "Great Vehicle" or "Great Path"). These teachings that arose in India some time between the first century B.C.E. and the first century C.E., emphasize benefiting others. They are sometimes even called the *"bodhisattvayana"* (the "bodhisattva vehicle" or "bodhisattva path"). The American-born Buddhist nun and well-known author, Pema Chödrön, has popularized many of the Mahayana teachings in her books, including *Start Where You Are: A Guide to Compassionate Living* and *No Time to Lose: A Timely Guide to the Way of the Bodhisattva.*

There is a story, perhaps apocryphal, that the founder of Naropa, Chögyam Trungpa, said that the aim of the contemplative psychotherapy program was to "train bodhisattvas." As a teacher within this program, I have discovered that the fears I had about the bodhisattva ideal when I first began to study the bodhisattva teachings were well-founded. These teachings ask us to go beyond the narrow outlook of what is usually called "ego" in Western presentations of Buddhism. As will be discussed in more detail in chapter 3, from the Buddhist point of view, we mistakenly hold on to a sense of self as solid, separate, and permanent. Practicing these teachings exposes this sense of self, this ego, for the illusion that it is. We are not who we think we are. What could be more threatening? Or annoying? Yet, what Buddhism teaches, and what my own experience indicates to be true, is that letting go of this false sense of self is in fact a path to delight, spontaneity, creativity, openness, and (so I have been told) liberation itself. The ongoing dance of letting go and holding on is part of the path of the training of the bodhisattva. By practicing working for the benefit of others, and putting the needs of others first, we begin to disengage from the snare of our habitual ego patterns. When we as mental health practitioners employ these teachings in the context of our counseling and psychotherapeutic work, our clinical work becomes contemplative practice, part of our spiritual path.

Shantideva expressed the wish to be anything someone might need on the journey to full awakening—but he probably didn't imagine our modern methods of intimate helping called psychotherapy and counseling. I have often thought what a strange thing psychotherapy is: as clients and patients, we seek out total strangers and pay them to be with us as we unburden our hearts to them. We speak of our deepest pain and secrets to people we have never met before. Perhaps we've heard a little about them from a trusted friend or doctor. Perhaps we have chosen them from a website based on what they've said about themselves, or how they look, or what brand of psychotherapy they espouse. Still, isn't it a bit odd?

In an earlier time, when change happened less quickly, we might have sought help with our confusion or pain from elders in the family or the community. These days, however, many of us have no extended family nearby: no great-aunts and uncles, no wise old men and women of the clan to whom we can turn. As we struggle with relationships that no longer follow traditional rules and roles, career choices that we no longer expect to last a lifetime, and decisions that seem to multiply daily, we may perhaps think that our elders wouldn't necessarily know how to help us even if they were nearby. Friends, too, may not always be helpful, because they are often our own age and struggling with similar issues.

It has become commonplace in the modern Western world to turn to professionals for the wisdom that at one time resided in our elders. For me, the teachings on the path of the bodhisattva are like hearing the wise counsel of an elder of the family. Paradoxically, these teachings by people in the distant past—people who never heard of psychotherapy, feminism, cell phones, electricity, or a host of other modern phenomena—provide me with insight into my own and my clients' dilemmas. Although our problems seem to be unique to our own time, they turn out to be, in many ways, timeless. Each time I turn to these teachings, or present them in class, I find new inspiration to go beyond my own self-centeredness, as well as practical advice for working with my own and others' suffering and confusion.

This book will explore the teachings on the path of the bodhisattva and, more specifically, their application to the work of psychotherapy and counseling, drawing on my work with many students and colleagues over the years in exploring that integration. The format of this book follows the development of an aspiring bodhisattva. Not surprisingly, it also parallels the unfolding of a therapeutic relationship. We will begin in part 1 with some theoretical orientation, by first familiarizing ourselves with the Mahayana Buddhist view of human nature, *bodhichitta* (Sanskrit for "awakened heart"; see chapter 1), and then going on to look at basic Buddhist teachings on the causes of our suffering and confusion and how they may be alleviated (chapters 2 through 5). Then we will look at a pivotal Mahayana teaching, on the nature of emptiness (chapter 6), before discussing some of the underlying principles of contemplative psychotherapy (chapter 7).

As therapists we begin our relationship with a new client by seeking to establish some kind of connection, or rapport; in this book, we will first cultivate such a connection with ourselves, through the sitting practice of meditation, which is introduced at the beginning of part 2 (chapter 8). As we get to know our clients better, we begin to understand their views of themselves and others. We come to understand why they have sought help, what resources they bring, what aspirations they have. In chapters 9 through 12, we will look into the teachings known as the "four immeasurables" or "limitless ones," which help us clarify and strengthen our own aspirations as bodhisattva-helpers.

Finally, in our professional relationships, we get to the heart of the matter with our clients, profoundly experiencing the wisdom and confusion of ourselves and our clients. In part 3 of this book, our deepening therapeutic engagement is presented through the teachings on the six "awakened" or "transcendent" actions (*paramitas*) of the bodhisattva. Throughout these final chapters we will explore our own development, its application to clinical work, and the possibility of helping clients develop these same qualities and ways of being.

Although I have generally employed English translations of Buddhist terms in the text, I have chosen to retain two Sanskrit terms. I have elected to use *bodhisattva* throughout the book since I haven't found an English version of it that I like, and I have used *bodhichitta* in many places in addition to the translation "awakened heart," since it, too, is not a term for which English has a really good equivalent. Throughout the book, the names of clients and the details of their lives have been changed to protect their privacy. Sometimes I have created composites of more than one client for the same reason.

While the teachings in this book are drawn from the Buddhist Mahayana tradition, there is no reason that one needs to be any sort of Buddhist at all to find them helpful. What I suggest to my students at Naropa is that they first just listen, read, and make an effort to understand what is being presented. Then, they should reflect on what they've learned; see if it makes sense to them. Talk about it with each other. If it makes sense, then they can begin to apply it in their own lives, test it out for themselves. I would suggest the same to the readers of this book. Perhaps these teachings will augment a tradition with which you are already deeply connected. Perhaps they will present you with a tradition into which you want to delve more deeply.

In any case, it is my deep wish to present the teachings of the path of the bodhisattva to you as well as I can while recognizing that I am a fellow traveler on the path. Any errors in understanding presented here are my own.

Part One
the path of awakening
natural wisdom

Just like a blindman
Discovering a jewel in a heap of rubbish,
Likewise by some coincidence
[Bodhichitta] has been born within me.

—*Shantideva,*
A Guide to the Bodhisattva's Way of Life[1]

1

the awakened heart of the bodhisattva

ELLIE WAS TELLING me about what it was like for her growing up. She remembered that she always felt afraid and that she often spent time hiding from people behind the sofa in the living room. However, it was only when she was an adult and her elderly mother told her the following story that Ellie got a clearer sense of why she had always been so afraid and lonely.

Ellie's mother described a warm southern afternoon when the family was sitting outside enjoying a few drinks. Ellie was an infant, just a few months old, and lay on a blanket under a shady tree. At one point she began to cry. No one made a move to see what was wrong. Then, as she continued to cry, her father took a switch and sat down next to her. "Whenever you cried, he'd switch you. You stopped soon enough," Ellie's mother told her. As she told the story, Ellie's mother laughed a bit and added, "He didn't really hurt you, you know." Ellie told me that she learned never to cry or call out for her mother.

As I listened to Ellie's story, I felt tremendous pain. I was horrified by a mother who could laugh about her infant child being struck and not see that it did hurt her; I was angry at this man who would hit a baby; I was brokenhearted for this infant and now this woman who still carried the scars of his unacknowledged cruelty. I found it difficult to tolerate this mixture of pain.

For psychotherapists and counselors, this is exactly what we have signed up for. We offer to go along with our clients as they explore their pain and learn how to work with it. In the contemplative approach, which we will look at in more detail in chapter 7, we do not try to distance ourselves from our clients' pain. I suspect that no matter what theoretical orientation a practitioner has, there is no escaping discomfort in our work. We may experience anguish while listening to our clients' pain; sometimes our clients become angry at us; sometimes we feel helpless and uncertain.

If someone had said to me when I was a young person, "Someday would you like to earn your living sitting down with people who are suffering and share their suffering?" I don't know that I would have said yes. If that someone had gone on and said, "Sometimes you would be able to help; sometimes you would just feel stupid and helpless. Often the results of your work would be unclear; you would never be sure of what you had or had not accomplished," I would hardly have felt enthusiastic about such a prospect.

DISCOVERING BODHICHITTA

Why *would* anyone want to do this kind of work? What does inspire us to become counselors and psychotherapists? It's not an inordinately lucrative profession; it is difficult and often personally disconfirming; it's not even glamorous. From the point of view of ego, it's completely crazy. There must be something in us that's stronger than ego—and from the Mahayana Buddhist perspective, that "something" is *bodhichitta,* the inherent and natural motivation we feel to alleviate the suffering of ourselves and others. Bodhichitta can be understood as having two aspects: we can speak of "absolute bodhichitta" and "relative bodhichitta."

Absolute Bodhichitta

In Buddhism, *absolute* refers to the way things actually are, while *relative* refers to how they appear or how we experience them. "Absolute bodhichitta" refers to our natural wisdom, which recognizes the truth of how things are. The experience of absolute bodhichitta is nonconceptual; it cannot be captured in words. Often translated as "awakened heart" or "awakened mind," absolute bodhichitta allows us to perceive the nature of ourselves and all phenomena as "empty," a topic we will look at more closely in chapter 6.

Perhaps the following example will suggest something of the nondual and nonconceptual nature of bodhichitta. My friend Philip and his wife, Sandra, recently had an infant daughter, Jessica. Philip described to me how difficult he was finding it to be wholeheartedly loving toward this child. His own experience growing up was of being alternately neglected and criticized. In addition, he was afraid that Sandra's devotion to the child would take away from the love she had been sharing with him. He was quite uncomfortable with both his halfheartedness and with his jealousy. "How can I offer love to a baby when I never experienced it myself from my own parents?" he wondered.

I offered a suggestion to him. "Maybe," I said, "you could pretend that the baby is also you as a child, and you could give her all the love you wish you had gotten." Philip looked skeptical but said he'd give it a try.

The next time I saw Philip, he was glowing. He had taken my suggestion and gone far beyond it. "When I held Jessica and tried to feel the love toward her that I wished I had gotten, the strangest thing happened. Something just opened up, and I felt filled with love. It wasn't just that I loved Jessica, I was just feeling love altogether. It's hard to describe, but when I felt that love, I got to feel loving and loved all at once. I was the love itself in that moment."

What Philip described was the experience of bodhichitta, or natural compassion, experienced as an expansive, nondual wisdom. In moments of experiencing this absolute bodhichitta, a person is able to perceive that compassion doesn't have to belong to anyone; it is not limited by the confines of ego or any ideas of separation between self and other. It is as though it is part of the air, the environment.

Relative Bodhichitta

Another aspect of bodhichitta is "relative bodhichitta," our aspiration to wake up so that we can benefit all beings. As the Buddhists would put it, we aspire to attain enlightenment or liberation so that we can actually do what it takes to truly alleviate suffering. Until we are fully awakened, we experience bodhichitta's relative aspect: the desire to awaken so that we could act in accordance with our natural wisdom, our absolute bodhichitta. Relative bodhichitta is further divided into two kinds: "aspiring" bodhichitta and "applying" or "active" bodhi- chitta. "Aspiring bodhichitta" is the desire (the thought, the inspira- tion) to benefit beings, and there are practices associated with it that we will explore later in part 2. "Applying bodhichitta," by contrast, is associated with actually beginning the work of helping others, which in this book is addressed in part 3.

As already noted, according to the Buddhist view, our minds are generally clouded by the distortion of ego-clinging. As a result, we are easily confused about what will help and what will make things worse. Therefore, we need to begin first with clarifying our own confusion. Only then can we act on our intention to be of help. Some Buddhists take this advice quite literally and go on multiyear meditation retreats to work with their own confusion before attempting to help others. My own teacher, Chögyam Trungpa, encouraged his students to work on their own minds but also to take a "leap" and work with others as well, and that is the view I am presenting here.

Connecting with Bodhichitta

I am always interested in how people connect with or "arouse" bodhi- chitta. When we interview applicants for Naropa's MA program in contemplative psychotherapy, we ask them why they want to become therapists. Often they have become inspired by seeing the deep suf- fering of someone close to them. I remember one woman who had a brother who struggled with debilitating bipolar symptoms. Her deepest wish was to know how to help him and others like him. Many applicants have recovered from addictive behaviors and wish to repay the kindness of those who had helped them; often that kindness has involved not only helping them to overcome their addictions but also helping them regain their self-respect.

A traditional way to arouse bodhichitta is to think of one's mother and all she did for us when we were helpless infants. We might con- template the endless diapers, the nighttime feedings, the runny noses, and realize how grateful we are for our mother's generosity. We then imagine that all beings have been our mothers, and we aspire to repay their kindness.

I have found, however, that this traditional contemplation doesn't work for many of my students. Like Ellie, they may have had difficult relationships with their mothers, and bodhichitta doesn't particularly arise when they think of her. Under these circumstances, other contemplations may be helpful. Some students prefer simply to think of someone else who cared for them: their father, a teacher, a relative. This helps them touch a quality of tenderness in themselves that they can then imagine extending to others.

Another gateway into bodhichitta is to think of someone we ourselves have cared for: a child or a pet, for instance. In the same way we would do anything for our beloved child or our suffering and helpless animal, we aspire to do whatever is needed for other beings.

One morning I woke up to find my elderly dog, Molly, sniffing near a bird in the backyard. It was a small crow, and it was squawking and walking up and down the walkway. I called the people from the local wildlife agency, who arrived quickly to deal with this bird that didn't seem able to fly. As they worked with the bird, gently washing its mouth clean from some kind of foamy stuff, two large crows showed up, cawing loudly and circling over us. These were this adolescent crow's parents, and they were expressing their concern very clearly. They followed as the wildlife officers carried the youngster up the road and placed it in a nearby tree. Then, they swooped down and joined it. Even crows have bodhichitta.

Chögyam Trungpa used to point out that everyone has a "soft spot" somewhere, even if it's just for their favorite food. And any "soft spot" can be a place to start in accessing our inherent compassion, first for ourselves and then for others. The idea is that all of us have a compassionate heart, although many of us have learned to cover it up.

A MAN CALLED THE BUDDHA

The man who has come to be known as the Buddha was born as a prince about twenty-five hundred years ago. The king, his father, like all fathers, wanted to protect his son from pain, and so he kept the prince walled up in the palace compound. The king also wanted to distract his son, whose name was Siddhartha, from any interest he might have in doing something other than becoming the king himself when the time came. Even though the king provided the young prince with all the luxury and entertainment he could possibly desire, Siddhartha was still curious about what went on outside the palace walls. As the story goes, he was able to convince his chariot driver to take him on a journey into the city outside the walls, where the evidence of poverty, old age, and sickness was readily apparent all around him. Having been shielded from the suffering of others his whole life, these sights were shocking to him. Siddhartha also saw a mendicant monk, a holy man who had dedicated himself to spiritual seeking. Unlike any other people whom the prince had seen before, this man seemed special. He was dignified and calm. (As I imagine this encounter, I think of inspiring people I have met in my life: people who emanate a sense of serenity, liveliness, and wisdom.) The prince felt very drawn to the qualities he saw in this spiritual seeker. Appalled by the suffering he had seen, the young prince resolved to leave his privileged life and dedicate himself to understanding the nature of suffering and its relief.

To make the rest of this long tale shorter, we can simply note that ultimately, by sitting down and observing his own direct experience, Siddhartha realized his true nature and penetrated to the causes of suffering. It was at that point that he became known as the Buddha, "the awakened one." For the rest of his long life, he taught what he had discovered to disciples, royal patrons, and common people. His teachings are known as the *dharma*, and the first teaching he gave addressed the concept of the "Four Noble Truths."

Like the Buddha, we are curious and want to understand our own and others' minds and experiences. Although we may distract ourselves, our bodhichitta impulses are strong, and as therapists we long to find skillful ways to work with the suffering we find in ourselves, in our clients, and in the wider world.

THE HINAYANA PATH

Not unlike other spiritual traditions—Christianity and Judaism, for example—Buddhism has within it a number of different schools and traditions. In the Tibetan tradition in which I was trained there are three main sets of teachings. The first of these is known as the *Hinayana* or "foundational vehicle." Without it our aspirations to be of help would be nothing more than fleeting ideas floating in air. The first thing we do on the Buddhist spiritual path is to become familiar with our own minds. We come to know, in great detail, exactly how our own minds work not by just by studying *about* them but by bringing our focused attention to our experience, particularly through the practice of mindfulness-awareness meditation (introduced in chapter 8). The foundational or Hinayana path, not to be confused with the Theravadin school of Buddhism, is also called the "narrow" vehicle, since we begin by narrowing our attention to our moment-to-moment experience.[1]

Where I live in Colorado, there are a number of beautiful narrow roads that go up into the mountain canyons. The Hinayana path reminds me of biking up the Left Hand Canyon Road, which parallels a mountain creek. It winds and twists along with the creek, which pours down from the mountains in the springtime. As I bike up the canyon road, I can't see very far ahead. I have to pay attention to what is immediately in front of me. The walls of the canyon are high and rocky. Around each bend is something new: a different tree, a different texture in the road, a new large boulder. It requires great attention and concentration to stay on the far right and not wander into the traffic of this very narrow road. The foundational path is like this, too. One pays close attention to all the details of one's experience as one sits on one's meditation cushion.

THE MAHAYANA PATH

Both historically and in the unfolding path of a particular practitioner, the narrow focus of the Hinayana path is followed by the expanded approach of the Mahayana teachings. The Mahayana path is like coming to the top of a mountain canyon road and turning around and looking back. The narrow roadway is replaced with an enormous vista over the plains. Suddenly, the view becomes enormous, breathtaking. Bodhichitta, which marks the entrance into the Mahayana, may feel just as startling and vast. We may recognize—for perhaps just a moment—that the world is filled with beings suffering just as we do. In that same moment the longing to relieve that suffering arises, without deliberation or thought. It is momentarily obvious that we can be much more open, much more heartfelt and expansive. As Shantideva points out in the passage cited at the start of this section of the book, the experience of bodhichitta is rare and unexpected. We are as likely to find it as a blind person is to find a diamond in a dumpster. Still, if we pay attention, we may discover the heart of bodhichitta in ourselves.

BODHISATTVA VOW

In the Buddhist tradition, people who dedicate themselves to cultivating bodhichitta and working for the benefit of all beings may choose to take "the bodhisattva vow."[2] In taking this vow, they pledge to progressively train themselves in the practices that will not only reduce their own confusion but also develop the qualities and skills that will relieve others' suffering. These are the people who are known as "bodhisattvas." Counselors and psychotherapists who are committed to working to alleviate the suffering of their clients may have a similar aspiration without taking a formal vow.

BODHICHITTA ORIENTATION

All counselors and psychotherapists base their work on some theoretical orientation. It may be psychoanalytic, cognitive-behavioral, contemplative, or any number of others. Part of any theoretical orientation is a view of human nature and a way of understanding how suffering arises and may be alleviated. Whatever our view is, it will determine what we pay attention to, how we understand what healing is, and also how we evaluate whether our work is successful.

We may have a view that holds, for example, that people are always thinking something and that some thoughts lead to depression and others lead to active engagement in life. If that's our view, it will direct our attention to what our clients think and how they deal with those thoughts. Cognitive-behavioral therapies, for example, help clients identify dysfunctional patterns of thinking that lead to depression and replace them with more beneficial thoughts.

In Mahayana Buddhism and likewise in contemplative psychotherapy, our view, our orientation, is that all beings have the potential described by "absolute bodhichitta." We are interested not only in our clients' pain and dysfunctional patterns but also in their inherent wisdom and compassion. Our task is to help our clients bring awareness and kindness to their own experience and to support them in seeing beyond their ego-limited views of themselves and their lives. The rest of this book explores the implications of such an orientation for counseling and psychotherapy.

GLIMPSING BODHICHITTA
IN OURSELVES AND IN OUR CLIENTS

Most of us do not live our lives in touch with our awakened hearts, our bodhichitta. Yet, we do have hints of it from time to time. We also recognize signs of its presence in our clients.

Sarah, a woman I worked with for a while, had struggled with depression most of her life. One aspect of depression for her was a sense that her life had no direction, no purpose, no meaning. As a result she had difficulty making decisions about her work, her living situation, and her relationships. We spent time together talking about what really mattered to her. Then, one day she came in and said, "Really, I just want to be a decent person. That's what matters."

Being "decent" for her was about treating others with kindness and consideration. It meant putting herself in another's place and trying to see what the world was like for the other person. Being a decent person became her orientation, her reference point for what to do and what not to do.

In one instance, for example, she had to decide whether to help her parents move. This was a difficult decision because they were quite critical of her. It was always challenging to be around them. At the same time, they were now quite elderly and had asked for her help. "What,"

Sarah asked herself, "is the decent thing to do here?" How could she behave decently with them and also with herself? She devised a plan that allowed her to go and help her parents move but that also built in support for herself through staying with friends, practicing yoga, and limiting the time of her visit. Having the reference point of decency has opened up a sense of direction for her and reflects her inherent awakened heart.

Another woman, Bethany, had long been diagnosed with major mental illness. She lived in a private mental world that she almost never revealed to others. One day, in an anguished voice, she said, "What about the children? Someone has to take care of the children!" I had no idea what children she might have been talking about: real children? imaginary children? herself as a child? There was no way to know, but it was clear that the children needed help and care and that Bethany was in pain contemplating their unmet needs. Even in the confusion of psychosis, bodhichitta may be glimpsed.

Bodhichitta is sometimes even more disguised. Evidence of bodhichitta may appear as irritation or impatience. I wanted my client Charlie to make a different choice from the one he made. Instead of letting go of a job that he hated and taking the risk to accept another one, he chose to keep the old one. I felt despairing—and annoyed. I was sure that I was right and that he was wrong. My feeling that Charlie would probably continue to suffer in his present job and that he could, perhaps, suffer less in a different situation was a glimpse of bodhichitta: I wanted him to suffer less. However, instead of allowing myself to feel the despair and helplessness that arose for me along with that insight, I turned it into the less vulnerable experience of annoyance. That is to say: underneath my irritation was the cool insight and tender compassion of bodhichitta, but on top was my desire to avoid feeling useless, and so I felt frustration and annoyance instead. Still, those unpleasant feelings were an indication of my underlying awakened heart.

One need look no further than the daily news to see that the world is filled with people behaving seemingly without compassion and without awareness. Still, the Buddhist view is that underneath the surface of all of our actions, there exists our inherent bodhichitta. Understanding how we lose touch with these natural capacities forms an important part of the training of a bodhisattva.

2
acknowledging suffering
the first noble truth

THE EARLIEST TEACHINGS of the Buddha emphasized looking into and working with our own situation, our own suffering, and our own minds, and are known as the Four Noble Truths. The Four Noble Truths follow the ancient Indian medical model of diagnosis, etiology, prognosis, and treatment, and the Buddha identified them as (1) the truth of suffering, (2) the truth of the origin of suffering, (3) the truth of the cessation of suffering, and (4) the truth of the path. These teachings are the foundation of all of the many different schools of Buddhism. The Four Noble Truths provide insight not only into how we lose touch with our inherent wisdom and compassion but also how we might connect with them again. In this chapter we will look at the First Noble Truth, which describes the nature of our confusion and suffering, and we will also discuss some implications these teachings have for counseling and psychotherapy. The Second Noble Truth, which describes how our confusion arises, will be discussed in chapter 3, along with the Buddhist teachings on "karma" and "dependent co-arising" and their roles in perpetuating suffering. In chapters 4 and 5, we will look at the Third and Fourth Noble Truths, which describe how we may become liberated from suffering and confusion.

DIAGNOSIS: THE TRUTH OF SUFFERING

The First Noble Truth, the diagnosis the Buddha made for the confusion and suffering he saw all around him, is very simple: suffering, or *duhkha,* is an unavoidable part of life.

Duhkha is sometimes translated as "unsatisfactoriness." Life, according to the Buddha, will never be completely satisfactory. The common dream of being fulfilled in all our desires, of being always happy and getting everything we want, will never come true. That's just how life is. There is, in the traditional formula, the pain of birth, old age, sickness, and death. According to the First Noble Truth, the first step in discovering truth and relieving our own and anyone else's suffering is to acknowledge the pain and suffering that are present in our lives. Sometimes people assume that Buddhism is a pessimistic sort of tradition because of this teaching. In fact, however, recognizing that pain is simply part of being alive can be a relief. It is not a sign that we have done something wrong, stupid, or shameful. Yet I often catch myself and hear others making just that assumption—that pain and suffering are signs of some personal defect.

If I tell one friend that I have a cold, for instance, she is likely to say, "Well, how did that happen? Were you out without your hat in the cold?" Even more distressing is the view we all have heard at one time or another, which blames sufferers of serious diseases for having them: "Oh, yes, cancer is a sign of unexpressed grief." Of course, as modern medical research is increasingly showing us, the mind and the body are deeply interconnected, and our attitudes, emotions, and behaviors do affect our health. Yet, even if we were able to do "everything right," if we live long enough, we will not escape old age, sickness, and death. Nonetheless, thinking that illness is something to be "battled" at all costs and seeing death as defeat are common ideas in the West.

THE THREE MARKS OF EXISTENCE

The Buddha taught that there are three characteristics that "mark" our existence. The three marks of existence are (1) impermanence, (2) egolessness, and (3) suffering. All three are things we tend to ignore or avoid.

The teaching on impermanence at first seems easy to understand, but it is hard to really grasp its implications. Simply put, everything is changing all of the time. We can easily see this in the environment:

the seasons change, the weather changes, day becomes night, and night is followed by day. In our bodies, too, everything is changing: we grow from infancy into childhood, adulthood, old age, and death. In our emotions and thoughts, too, there is constant change. Feelings of well-being may be replaced by sadness, followed perhaps by anger, jealousy, or delight.

A further implication of impermanence is the second mark of existence: egolessness, the idea that our very sense of ourselves is also changing. Buddhism teaches that there is no permanent self in our being. This, too, is not a difficult concept to understand, yet it is quite difficult to let go of our ideas about who we think we are.

The third mark of existence, suffering, is (as we have already noted) an aspect of being alive that we may have particular difficulty acknowledging. In fact, I have noticed that many therapists, myself and others, are especially likely to offer to listen to others' troubles but to minimize our own. When we do this, we are expressing denial of this characteristic of existence; we are avoiding the truth of suffering.

TYPES OF SUFFERING

A final important aspect of the First Noble Truth is the difference between the direct experience of discomfort on one hand and how we react to it on the other hand. Sometimes the former is called "pain," and the latter is called "suffering." In her book *Everyday Zen: Love and Work*, Charlotte Joko Beck, an American Zen teacher who began teaching Buddhism in the 1980s, called the first one "true suffering" and the second "false suffering."[1]

The point is that we cannot escape feeling the sometimes sharp sting of pain. If we stub our toe, it hurts. A broken arm hurts. Grief hurts. On top of that pain though, we load on lots of thoughts and additional emotions. We struggle with the pain and try to get rid of it. We spend a lot of energy and time in trying to avoid, reduce, or even deny our pain. From the Buddhist point of view, all of this extra struggle and these attempts to escape from pain cause even more discomfort (as we will explore in chapter 3, which discusses the Second Noble Truth). The struggle to escape the already-present experience of pain is, in itself, suffering. Many who cope with chronic pain have reached a similar conclusion. If we are willing to just feel the pain that is here, we suffer less. This doesn't mean that we never take an aspirin or that we avoid medical treatment. It suggests, rather, that we could deal with pain first, and sometimes best, by acknowledging what is happening and not becoming overwhelmed by our emotions and thoughts about what might happen in the not-yet-here future.

SOME CLINICAL IMPLICATIONS OF THE THREE MARKS OF EXISTENCE

Usually clients seek counseling or psychotherapy because they are experiencing one of the three marks of existence: impermanence, egolessness, or suffering.

Impermanence

Many times clients come in because they are in transition. Perhaps someone important to them has died or is ill. Perhaps they have experienced an important loss: a relationship, a job, an ability they had before. They may be in the midst of a divorce or about to become married. It is not uncommon that initial psychotic breaks occur at transition points, often at the end of high school or during the beginning of college. All of these reflect the mark of impermanence.

Egolessness

Clients also seek out help when they experience a shock to their sense of who they believe they are. I remember one young man who came to see me: Jim was a sophomore in college, about nineteen years old. He had been playing basketball one day with some friends, and suddenly he wasn't sure who he was. It was as though he had suddenly woken up and found himself on a basketball court and didn't know what he was doing there. Intense anxiety arose, and he concluded that something was seriously wrong with him. He quickly made an appointment with a therapist.

Jim found his mind reeling. Was he someone who even liked basketball? If not, then was he still Jim? He didn't use exactly these words, but this was the gist of his problem. His definition of himself had suddenly shattered. When I suggested that maybe he was changing and that what he wanted to do was also changing, he was deeply relieved. Just knowing that he didn't have to maintain the same story about himself was really all he needed to hear.

A glimpse of egolessness can feel like a jolt from the blue, as it did for Jim. Retiring from a job that has defined us can also be such a shock. Becoming a parent or having one's children leave home and becoming an "empty nester" are other times when we may experience egolessness. At a much more subtle level, we may have an insight that there isn't anything in us that corresponds to an unchanging "me." Any of us, including our clients, may respond to such an experience with anxiety, anger, or depression.

Suffering

The third mark of existence, suffering, is the primary reason people arrive at counseling or therapy. Denying the first two marks, impermanence and egolessness, leads to suffering, but there may be other reasons clients experience pain and seek out help. As therapists, often one of our first tasks is to help clients acknowledge the pain and suffering they are experiencing. Instead of becoming caught up in the details of the stories they tell about why they are in pain, or who else is to blame for it, we can be interested in their direct experience. We need to watch out for our own tendency to avoid pain, which can manifest as jumping in too quickly to explain, prematurely diagnose, make suggestions, or otherwise interfere in clients' experience in the moment.

3

why are we so confused?

the second noble truth

WE SAW IN CHAPTER 2 that the first step in being able to recognize and cultivate our awakened heart, our inherent bodhichitta, is to acknowledge the pain and suffering in our lives. In this chapter, we will look at the Second Noble Truth, which describes the cause of our suffering and confusion.

ETIOLOGY: THE TRUTH OF THE ORIGIN OF SUFFERING

The Second Noble Truth is the truth of the origin, or cause, of suffering. According to the Buddha, we suffer because, in our confusion, we make the same mistake over and over again. That mistake is to take our ever-changing flow of experience and grasp on to it as a solid, separate, and permanent sense of self, or "ego." We then mindlessly hang on to this false sense of self with tenacity and vigor. The term *ego* is used here in this very specific Buddhist sense. Other uses of the term, such as the ability to know one's experience, to use logic, or to feel confident, are not regarded as problems. It is, perhaps, unfortunate that the same term is often used for all of these meanings.

EGO AND EGOLESSNESS

From the Buddhist point of view, ego does not actually exist and never has. It manifests as belief, but even more commonly, it is more of a gut feeling. Believing that ego is solid means that we think that we have some essential core that is not made up of component parts. Regarding ourselves as separate reflects our conviction that we exist independently of others and our environment. Finally, the notion of permanence suggests that there is something in us that does not change.

According to Buddhist teachings, however, we have nothing indivisible or unchanging in us. Furthermore, we do not exist independently, but interdependently. To use Thich Nhat Hanh's term from his book *Being Peace,* we "inter-are."[1] For example, my body is made up of cells, which are themselves made up of smaller components. My thoughts arise in a particular language and contain images, words, and concepts I have learned. The particular arrangement is unique in the moment, but it is also impermanent. Emotions, too, lack any solidity. As we will see in later chapters, our emotions do not arise independently; we are always "exchanging" with others in the environment. For example, if I am with an angry friend, I may begin to feel the signs of anger in my own body, emotions, and mind.

There are more detailed traditional teachings on the question of egolessness, and I've made suggestions for further study at the end of this book if you are interested in pursuing this more deeply.

THE PROBLEM WITH EGO

The problem with having this sense of ego is that, since it is not real, we have to spend a great deal of energy and attention on its maintenance while at the same time not recognizing that any such maintenance is required. Since ego has no ultimate reality, it keeps falling apart and our true situation, egolessness, keeps revealing itself.

Glimpses of egolessness are quite inconvenient from ego's point of view. We maintain ego with internal narratives, or "story lines," and with what are known as the "three poisons." These poisons are passion, aggression, and ignorance. Passion refers to hanging on to whatever supports ego; aggression is rejecting whatever threatens it; and ignorance is simply not noticing anything that neither supports nor threatens ego. We elaborate these three emotional primary colors into complex emotional dramas. Most of us are quite skilled in creating believable stories to sustain our sense of ego and are resistant to anything that causes us to question these stories.

When I went to my fifteenth high school reunion many years ago, I ran into Johnny, a man I had known since kindergarten. I remember going to Johnny's sixth birthday party. I was just delighted to see him and was enjoying our conversation and reminiscences until he said, "Karen, I'm so glad you're not still mad about what I said at the prom." The thirty-three-year-old man sitting in front of me was suddenly again the eighteen-year-old who had said something unkind. I instantly became angry. I didn't actually recall exactly what he'd said, but I was sure that if I was remembering how mad I was, I must have had a good reason. The anger I experienced at the reunion was uncomfortable and completely replaced the delight I had previously been enjoying, but I had resolidified the relationship between Johnny and myself, and I wasn't willing to let go.

SOME CLINICAL IMPLICATIONS OF THE SECOND NOBLE TRUTH

As therapists, if we are attentive to how our clients create and maintain ego and its story lines, we vividly see how the process of ego leads to suffering.

We can help our clients to see how they cause themselves unnecessary pain in this way, and we can also help them to recognize when and how these same stories fall apart. The falling apart can reveal a moment of egolessness.

Tracking Stories that Maintain Ego

Trying to maintain an unworkable definition of oneself is often the problem a client is struggling with. Needing to do everything "perfectly" is a common example. Another is trying to live up to an outmoded way of being, often learned in childhood. Adult children of alcoholics, for example, often perpetuate a role they played in their family of origin: perfect child, caretaker, rebel. These become ego-stories and so are quite difficult to let go. Without the old story, one has to experience the groundlessness of egolessness, uncertainty, openness.

A related ego-story that we see quite commonly in psychother-apy is self-aggression. First, any version of ego is a subtle form of self-aggression: we are rejecting our true nature and choosing to hold on to a false sense of ourselves. Self-aggression is a pervasive problem in Western society. We are bombarded with messages about how we don't look right, smell right, conduct our relationships properly, think the wrong thoughts, and so on. The media are filled with suggestions about how we ought to improve. These can range from the subtle to the blatant. In any case, I often see clients who believe quite deeply that they are basically bad. We will examine how to work with this common ego-story further in chapter 9, on loving-kindness, the anti-dote to self-aggression.

Recognizing Gaps in Ego's Story

Just when we have a good story line going about who we are and how we relate to the world, something may come along and interfere with our view. For example, many of us have had an experience similar to my client Sal's.

Sal was in a heated argument with his partner. "You said that you would make dinner tonight. I come home from work, exhausted and hungry, and you haven't done a thing. You don't really care about me. I don't know what to think! Maybe this whole relationship is a big mistake!"

The volume of Sal's partner's voice rose in response. "How can you say that! I do everything for you, and do you appreciate it? I told you I had a meeting tonight. You said that you would take care of dinner. I hate that you're always so self-centered. Do you even listen to what I tell you!"

The argument went on in this fashion, with each partner getting louder and more certain. Then, suddenly, Sal had a memory of agree-ing to make dinner! Oops!

In that moment of "oops!" Sal realized that he had fabricated the whole thing. It was very tempting to just bulldoze over the "oops" moment and keep the argument going. To do so would preserve pride and ego. To see the gap in the story line was to recognize a moment of emptiness, egolessness. Personally, I have chosen both options in my life plenty of times. And you?

KARMA AND INTERDEPENDENT ARISING

An important foundational teaching in Buddhism is the idea of karma. I have put it here with the teachings on the origin of suffering because it helps us to understand how we perpetuate dysfunctional, painful patterns in our lives. Karma means "action," and the teachings on karma are about actions and their consequences. According to the "laws" of karma, all positive actions lead to positive consequences, and all negative actions lead to negative consequences. Positive actions are those that benefit ourselves and others by awakening our inherent bodhichitta and helping us to develop wisdom and compassion. Negative actions are those that cause pain and suffering and lead to deeper confusion. Please note that karma is not the same thing as fate. From the point of view of karma, things do not happen randomly but are, instead, the result of our own choices and actions.

How does this work? In traditional Buddhist understanding, these consequences might not appear until later lifetimes. We are told that only a fully awakened, or enlightened, person can understand the workings of karma. Still, the basic idea can have power for us even without considering the possibility of past or future lives. The consequences of positive and negative actions bear fruit in the minds of their performer, sometimes quite immediately. Shantideva taught that when we act in a beneficial way, we experience happiness; when we act in a harmful way, we suffer.[2] We can experiment with this for ourselves.

A teaching closely related to the teaching about karma is that of "interdependent arising" (Sanskrit, *pratitya samutpada*). This teaching says that whatever we experience is the result of the coming together of many causes and conditions. "Causes" refers to the consequences of our actions, while "conditions" refers to generally seemingly external events. Each time we perform a particular sort of action, have a particular emotional experience, or generate a particular thought or mind-state, we "plant the seeds" of a similar experience in what has been described as the "storehouse consciousness" (Sanskrit, *alaya-vijnana*).

When that seed "ripens" and comes together with similar condi-tions, we feel something very like the original experience that we had when the seed was planted. For example, when I was a very little girl, I had seen a key that my older sister had. Oh, I wanted to have a key myself! Then I saw a big key lying on the walkway by the side of the house. With great delight, I picked it up, and it uncoiled itself to reveal that it was a worm! Ick! It was slimy and moving! I drew back in hor-ror. To this day, I react with horror to worms that appear suddenly. It has put a real crimp in my gardening aspirations. Each time I react in this way, I plant the seeds of continuing to react to worms and other creepy-crawlies in the same way.

SOME CLINICAL IMPLICATIONS
OF KARMA AND INTERDEPENDENT ARISING

The teachings of karma and interdependent arising have several impor-tant implications related to counseling and psychotherapy. First, quite simply, supporting our clients in performing positive actions will help them to feel better. Encouraging them to follow whatever inclina-tions they have in that direction can be quite powerful. One client of mine has discovered, for example, that when she volunteers at a local community agency, she feels good. She likes feeling helpful and useful. Helping clients refrain from harmful, negative behaviors such as mindless overeating or obsessively self-critical thinking, also may have positive results in a couple of ways. Whatever they do instead may have positive results, and refraining from something harmful also prevents the arising of negative consequences of the behavior that was not indulged.

Second, the teachings on interdependent arising emphasize the idea that all experiences have many causes and conditions that all come together. As counselors and therapists, we need to look beyond simple cause-and-effect relationships, and we need to help our cli-ents to do the same. In addition to challenging a familiar way of being (ego), asking a client to try out even a simple new behavior may have far-reaching consequences. Family therapists are familiar with this notion from systems theory, which emphasizes the fact that all the different parts of a family are interdependent, and a change made by one member can reverberate through the whole family system. So it is, too, for individual clients and their intrapersonal and interpersonal worlds. A change in one area will probably affect many others.

Third, an especially important consequence of understanding how seeds are planted in the storehouse consciousness and how they arise into awareness applies to our clinical work with trauma survivors. Each time clients think of an abusive event or a traumatic experience, they are creating the conditions that invite into awareness the seeds planted at the time of the original traumatic event. Moreover, this present experience of recalling the original event plants still more seeds that will ripen and arise in time. So, for example, when we attempt to help clients find release from the pain and suffering associated with early sexual abuse by encouraging them to remember the abuse, these memories may instead plant still more seeds of pain. We are "retraumatizing" our clients when we do this. As an alternative to planting more seeds of pain, however, we can consider helping our clients to "plant good seeds," to use Thich Nhat Hanh's expression.[3] Part of the power of the therapeutic relationship is exactly this. When clients recall painful events, we can encourage them to be in relationship with us in that moment, to bring mindfulness and kindness to themselves and to ground themselves in the reality of the nonthreatening present. In that way, they plant seeds of connection, mindfulness, kindness, and wakefulness. Although there are a great many therapists who believe that all past traumatic memories must be brought into the light of consciousness, Thich Nhat Hanh has even suggested that sometimes good seeds can take care of the "bad" seeds in the storehouse consciousness, without additional remembering being needed.

Having understood something about the pervasiveness of pain and suffering and how it arises, we naturally want to know what to do about it. If trying to avoid suffering causes more of it, what are we to do?

4
beyond suffering
the third noble truth

ACCORDING TO THE BUDDHA, we can stop perpetuating the cycle of death and rebirth, characterized by suffering, that the Buddhists call *samsara*. Even if we don't believe in repeated rebirths, we may still find his teachings on ending suffering valuable. It is possible, he taught, to realize the wakefulness and compassion described in the Mahayana teachings on bodhichitta.

PROGNOSIS: THE TRUTH
OF THE CESSATION OF SUFFERING

As we have seen, the direct experience of discomfort, "pain," is not the same as the struggle against it, which we have been calling "suffering." The Third Noble Truth is the truth of the cessation of suffering. Cessation of suffering means we can interrupt the habitual patterns, which keep planting the seeds of confusion and suffering. According to the teachings on karma and interdependent arising, which we explored in chapter 3, each time we experience or do anything, we plant seeds in the storehouse consciousness. Then, those seeds get "watered" by similar circumstances at a later point in time, and we find ourselves mindlessly feeling and acting in similar ways. It is these patterns of repetition that the Third Noble Truth addresses. Moreover, we can see through the illusion of ego and rest in the natural compassion of our awakened heart, our bodhichitta nature. The cessation of suffering doesn't mean we won't experience pain. In fact, the more awake we become, the more vividly we experience everything, including pain. One traditional teaching says that at the beginning of the spiritual path, pain feels like a hair on the palm. In the middle, it feels like a hair on the tongue, and at the end it feels like a hair in the eye. When I think of this description, I sometimes wonder why I would pursue such a path! And yet that longing to not lie to myself, to know the truth, and to alleviate unnecessary suffering keeps reasserting itself.

OUR INCLINATION TO WAKE UP

An aspect of our inherent bodhichitta is just this persistent inclination toward waking up. Because bodhichitta is even more fundamental than our confusion, it keeps showing up. We *can* go beyond our habits of confusion. Ego, and its resulting emotional dramas, can be seen through. As these two obstacles become less and less thick (through the practices that will be described in the next chapter, with the description of the Fourth Noble Truth), bodhichitta shines forth more and more clearly.

One way of talking about the Third Noble Truth that I especially like is the notion of "nowness." Instead of being caught up with thoughts about the past or worries about the future, Buddhism emphasizes the present moment: right here, right now. It is a deceptively simple idea. Nothing else is real, only now. When I began my meditation practice, I was shocked to see how little of my time was spent in the present moment.

When we are willing to be present, we tap into direct experience: that is, experience that is not filtered through our thoughts, expectations, hopes, and fears. Instead, we see, hear, taste, touch phenomena, and recognize thoughts and images in the mind without adding judgments or preferences. Things are just what they are. Putting nowness and direct experience together means being awake in the present moment. This is such a straightforward notion that it is practically simpleminded. And yet, it is difficult for most of us to let things be just what they are.

Often, instead of tapping in to our direct experience, we substitute concepts. An exercise we sometimes do in one of my classes at Naropa University to highlight this phenomenon involves mindful eating. Many Buddhist teachers encourage their students to try this exercise on a regular basis. In class, we might take a tangerine and begin by silently looking at it. We examine the texture, color, and shape of the particular piece of fruit in front of us. We pick it up and notice what it feels like in the hand. We might hold it up to our ear and see what sounds occur as we roll it in our fingers. Slowly, we begin to peel it. We sniff and notice its aroma. When thoughts arise of past tangerines or imaginings about how this one will taste, we notice them and let them go, by coming back to this tangerine in this moment. Carefully, but not *too* carefully, we separate out a section, and taking our time, we bring it to our mouth. We continue the exercise by noticing the spontaneous preparations that the mouth takes as the section of tangerine approaches. Then we taste it as if we've never tasted a tangerine before—and in fact, we never have tasted *this* tangerine before. We continue in this way until we've eaten the entire tangerine, letting each moment be unique.

This exercise highlights not only the details of the present moment of eating a tangerine; it also reveals, often rather pointedly, how often we miss the present moment. All too often, instead of tasting the tangerine, we taste our ideas about it. For example, I "know" that I don't like tangerines. I even have good reasons for my distaste: tangerines are acidic, they sting my chapped lips in the winter, they can be messy. However, if I just do the above exercise, and taste a particular tangerine, it is quite different from my mental tangerine. You might like to try this exercise for yourself.

SOME CLINICAL IMPLICATIONS OF THE THIRD NOBLE TRUTH

The Third Noble Truth directs the therapist's attention to what is happening right now in the therapeutic encounter, both for the therapist and also for the client. When we bring our attention to the present moment, we may find that both we and our clients tune in to our direct experience and natural wisdom.

Offering Undistracted Attention

To begin with, simply being present with my clients is probably the most valuable thing I can offer them. We live in a time when the invitation to be distracted from the present moment is especially strong. Cell phones, MP3 players, the Internet, satellite and cable TV, and so on, all offer innumerable possibilities to forget where we are and what we are doing. No doubt other technological challenges to remembering ourselves will be coming along soon.

Being able to offer my clients undistracted attention is a rarer gift than it used to be. Simply being with someone else and feeling recognized and heard is a relief for any of us. It lets us relax and recognize what our experience actually is. Therapy provides an occasion when both therapist and client can focus on direct experience. It gives us a chance to slow down and let go of our habitual speediness enough to do some self-scrutiny and see "how we really are."

The Opportunity to Connect with Direct Experience

I have worked with a number of clients in recent years whose main complaint is the urgency they are always feeling to get from one thing to the next. They feel overwhelmed and pressured by all of the demands on their seemingly shrinking time. In response, they go faster, eat more fast food, sleep less, and see their partners mostly as they pass in the doorway. They suffer with a sense of missing their lives, and, indeed, that is what is happening. Only rarely do they feel like they are where they are; they barely recognize a pleasant moment before they are rushing to get to the next thing on their list.

When they come into my office and give themselves the opportunity to slow down and simply be present, they often feel relief and sadness. For a moment or two, they drop the struggle to be somewhere else. They notice feelings that they have ignored, and often just recognizing what they are feeling is enough to show them what really needs to be done and what can be let go. Recognizing and letting go of the distractions from their direct present experience is, in itself, helpful.

For artists—writers, painters, musicians, and other creative people—a connection with direct experience is usually an important aspect of their art. But both artists and nonartists benefit from learning to tune in to direct, nonconceptual experience. The Third Noble Truth suggests that the awakened state of mind is always available; it is merely covered up with our habitual habits of clinging to a nonexistent ego. As therapists, we can have confidence in our clients' potential wisdom and compassion. Our job is one of uncovering and helping nurture qualities that are already present in our clients.

At the same time, having a healthy respect for ego's creation of confusion, and our addiction to it, is important, too. I remember a client who once stormed out of my office threatening to kill herself by driving into a tree. I had called the police and given them her car's license number. After the incident, when she had calmed down, she wanted me to promise that I would never again call the authorities about her. I told her I couldn't make that promise.

"Don't you trust me?" she asked.

"No," I said. "I don't trust anybody's confusion." To my surprise, she agreed that confusion was never to be trusted. Instead, she vowed that she would never give me a reason to call the police again. That was fine with me, and I hoped she was right.

Recognizing Natural Wisdom

Finally, an important implication of the Third Noble Truth has to do with recognizing the expressions and manifestations of our clients' underlying wisdom and compassion. It is quite tempting, I find, to focus on confusion. It is easier to describe and identify. We can even classify it neatly into various diagnostic categories. Recognizing our clients' natural wisdom, by contrast, can be more challenging, since it is not reducible to words or concepts. Yet, if we have learned to recognize our own glimpses of bodhichitta, we are better able to recognize inherent wisdom in our clients.

5
the path
the fourth noble truth

THE BUDDHA TAUGHT that there is a path, a gradual journey, that must be undertaken if we are to wake up from our habitual confusion. The Fourth Noble Truth is the truth of the path. This path is not already paved and ready for us to step onto it. Instead, the Buddhist path is one that we make ourselves as we go along. The Buddha provided guidelines about how to proceed, but it is up to us to create our own journey. Another way of understanding the idea of path is that it unfolds as we travel along it. In any case, the path doesn't exist until we set out upon it.

TREATMENT:
THE TRUTH OF THE PATH

Different Buddhist traditions describe the path in various ways, and the original teaching refers to it as the Eightfold Path. In the Tibetan tradition in which I have trained, the emphasis is on three aspects of the path: discipline, meditation, and wisdom.

Whichever version of Buddhism we choose to study, the essential quality of the path is bringing mindfulness and awareness to all aspects of our lives: actions of body, expressions of speech, and arisings of mind. Nothing is left out. In the Eightfold Path, for example, "right livelihood" is one of the eight aspects. Not only is it important that we earn our living, it is important that we do so in a way that does not harm others. Moreover, as we do our work, whatever it is, we bring attentiveness to each moment. In that way, our work is part of our spiritual path.

From that point of view, there is no distinction between activities that are spiritual and those that are not. There are practices taught in different traditions that help us to be awake to whatever we are doing. I particularly appreciate some of Thich Nhat Hanh's teachings on how to bring mindfulness to such mundane activities as sitting at a red light or answering a phone call.[1] Sitting at a red light, for example, gives us an opportunity to notice our breath, to come once again into a present, unique moment. Instead of being an interruption in our headlong momentum to get where we think we have to be, a red light lets us relax and simply be present. It becomes an opportunity to feel nourished and alive.

The Buddhist teachings on the path provide guidelines about what activities to cultivate and what to refrain from. In the Hinayana teachings, the emphasis is on refraining from harming others. For example, in terms of actions of body, we are told to not kill, steal, misuse intoxicants, or harm others through sexual misconduct. Similarly, we are instructed to bring mindfulness to all the activities of speech and mind. In the Mahayana teachings, not only are we required to refrain from harming others, but we are encouraged to cultivate the qualities that will enable us to actively benefit our fellow beings.

Traditionally, we find guidance and support from the example of the Buddha as a teacher, from the dharma (the teachings of the Buddha), and from the *sangha* (the community of fellow practitioners). Paradoxically, even though we recognize that we are not separate (as we saw above, in our discussion of ego), we are still alone in applying the teachings to our own experience.

SPIRITUAL MATERIALISM

A major obstacle on the path is what Chögyam Trungpa called "spiritual materialism."[2] Spiritual materialism is a distortion of the path. Instead of using the teachings to help us wake up from the delusion of ego and its resulting confusion, we misuse the teachings to further support ego. We might, for example, take great pride in having a particular teacher or being part of some spiritual community. We might even be competitive: "I'm in the best group!" This feeds our sense of ego rather than helping us see that ego is just a mistaken idea.

More problematic, as well as less obvious, is the misuse of spiritual practice by using it as a tool for becoming something other than who and what we are. In our attempts to be better, different, more spiritual, or even more compassionate, we subtly reject who we are now. This is a form of self-aggression and is ego activity all over again. It is a problem, not a solution. As we try to be new and improved versions of ourselves, we are seeking to fabricate a new and better ego.

How do we deal with this? It's a bit challenging. After all, if we didn't have some aspiration to be different from how we are, we wouldn't seek out meditation or other spiritual practices at all. Spiritual materialism is one of the last things we drop as we mature on the spiritual path. If we try not to indulge in spiritual materialism, that is just more spiritual materialism. What we can do, instead, is simply bring our mindfulness to anything that arises in our experience, including spiritual materialism and any other ego activity. In that way, everything becomes part of the path.

SOME CLINICAL IMPLICATIONS OF THE FOURTH NOBLE TRUTH

As all therapists know, therapy is a journey with its own beginning, middle, and end. While the therapeutic path, like the Buddhist path, also unfolds rather than following a set plan, there are different aspects of the therapeutic relationship we attend to as we go along. For example, we may begin the relationship by attending more to building trust than getting into the nitty-gritty details of a client's pain. We may refrain from making challenging direct statements until we have reason to believe that our client is ready for such things in the context of our relationship. We will probably talk about the ending of the relationship as we near termination in a way that we wouldn't at the beginning, and so on.

Avoiding Premature Interventions

The Second Noble Truth contains the idea that rejecting our experience in the present moment is a source of suffering. We will want, then, to be mindful of our attempts to bring an attitude of materialism into our clinical work. We may, and sometimes probably do, subtly and not so subtly push away the pain a client may need to explore in a particular therapy session. In our desire to alleviate suffering, we may try to skip over our own or a client's experience of pain. When we do that, we miss seeing what's actually happening and how it works.

For example, quickly jumping in with a technique to help an anxious client slow down, by focusing on her breathing, might abort her opportunity to see how she is feeding her fear in the moment. Student therapists are perhaps more likely to do this, but we are all quite capable of it. The message to the client may be, "Get rid of that experience of anxiety as soon as possible." Moreover, we are conveying to our clients that anxiety is not something that should be experienced directly. In this fashion, rather than being helpful we are supporting the attitude that leads to suffering: attempting to escape the inevitable pain of being alive.

This doesn't mean that we don't help clients to deal with pain, but it does mean that we don't try to solve a problem we don't yet understand. Perhaps, too, if the client lets herself feel the pain, she will be less frightened of it and more able to allow the experience to arise and dissipate on its own, as the teachings on impermanence suggest that it will.

Titrating Intensity

Another important aspect of the path is that it is gradual. Learning to refrain from causing our own suffering takes time, for the spiritual practitioner, the psychotherapist, and for the therapy client.

Many times the idea of a gradual path means that we will help our clients titrate the intensity of their painful experiences so that they can more easily stay present. Instead of encouraging our clients to feel extreme levels of fear, for example, we help them gradually touch into increasingly challenging degrees of fear. Fritz Perls, the founder of Gestalt therapy, described the benefit of creating a "safe emergency"—a level of tension in the moment that was neither too intense and paralyzing nor too dull and static.[3] We might, for example, raise the tension by asking a client to say something directly to us or lower it by asking them to merely imagine saying it instead. In this way, we find a way to progress step by step over time.

Recognizing Why Change Takes Time

One reason for keeping in mind that change is a gradually unfolding process is that, as we have seen, we have planted lots of seeds in the storehouse consciousness. Even when we know a pattern really well, seeds will continue to rise into consciousness. Clients often feel discouraged when an old pattern or feeling emerges again. "I thought I'd already dealt with that! I guess I'm still stuck in the same old place. I'm hopeless." Clients may very well have learned how to deal with a particular issue and its accompanying emotions, yet seeds will continue to sprout when the right causes and conditions come together. It takes a long time for such seeds to become "exhausted." If we understand that, we can help our clients work skillfully with such occasions, by pointing out what is happening and encouraging them to bring curiosity and even warmth to these experiences. We can help them plant new, more helpful, seeds.

Finally, in the same way that the Eightfold Path teaches us to bring mindfulness to all aspects of our lives, as therapists we need to view anything that happens in session with a client as being relevant. Instead of regarding a client's story about a trip to the movies, for example, as an attempt to avoid the issue at hand, we can help him pay attention to what he experiences when he tells the movie narrative. How is it different from what he experienced as he shared a story about a disagreement with his partner? We can work with anything in the moment. We could become curious about a pattern of movie-telling that seems to follow other kinds of stories. In any case, we can help our clients to extend their curiosity to all aspects of their lives.

Now that we have looked at the basic Buddhist teachings on how suffering arises and how it may be alleviated, let us turn to the profound and provocative Mahayana teaching on emptiness, which expands even further our understanding of how ego-clinging leads to suffering.

6
emptiness is not nothingness

IT IS SAID that when the Buddha presented the teachings on emptiness to his followers, some of them had heart attacks. The early teachings of the Buddha on interdependence implied that there were some actual things that were really "there." That is, there were some things that couldn't be broken down into smaller component parts. These small things could combine and recombine into all sorts of aggregates that were themselves impermanent and not solid, but these little things were real. There was something that could be counted on.

When the Buddha gave the discourse on emptiness known as the Heart Sutra, however, he proclaimed that there wasn't anything at all that was real in that way. According to this discourse, all phenomena are "empty."

WHAT IS EMPTINESS?

What does that mean? To say that things are empty is to say that they are not what we think they are. They are empty of our thoughts, our concepts, and any language we might apply to them. We cannot reduce the flow of experience to discrete pieces of any kind.

Sometimes when I teach about emptiness, I use my hair as an example. I have always identified myself as a redhead; as a child I had strawberry blonde hair. One day not long ago, I was participating in a group meditation retreat in New York State. I happened to look into the mirror over the sink. "Hmm," I thought, "in this light, my hair looks light brown." I quickly reassured myself, "But it's really red. It's just the poor light in here."

Then it occurred to me that there was no "really" about the color of my hair. It was always dependent upon causes and conditions: the light, the condition of my health and vision, how recently I'd been to the hairdresser to have it "brightened."

In the same way as my hair has no "really," neither do I. There is no "really" to who I am. That, too, depends on the coming together of causes and conditions in the moment.

It gets even worse. All of those causes and conditions are themselves empty of any "really." The Buddhist teaching on emptiness says that we cannot find anything at all that is free of this kind of interdependence. We can never pin down anything as, to use a Buddhist term, "truly existent." To be truly existent would mean that something or someone existed in a solid, permanent way without being dependent upon anything else. The Buddhist view here is that nothing exists separately from its interdependent nature. All that comes together is changing and in the process of falling apart again.

This is not different from what we saw in the teachings on the three marks of existence, but it takes us further. Everything we experience is empty of any true existence of any kind; there are no little particles to be found. Modern physics has reached a similar conclusion when it points out that at the most minute level, reality sometimes acts like a particle and sometimes like a wave, depending on how it is being perceived.

Instead of perceiving some real, external phenomenal world, what we experience are our own mental constructions. It would be easy to mistake this teaching as nihilism and think that nothing exists at all. This is not the Buddhist view. Buddhism regards nihilism as an error. In the Heart Sutra, the Buddha taught that "form is emptiness and emptiness is form." That is, even the idea of emptiness is a form, a concept. We may very well try to turn that into something real, too. Even emptiness is empty of our ideas about it.

The Buddhist teachings are known as the Middle Way. Buddhism rejects the two extreme views: either that things exist in a solid, permanent way (eternalism) or that they don't exist at all (nihilism). Instead the Buddhist teachings regard the existence of things as dependent on conditions, and so they speak of "dependent truth" or "relative truth." In contrast, "absolute truth" refers to that which does not exist dependent on any particular conditions or circumstances. In the Mahayana teachings, "absolute truth" refers to absolute bodhichitta, as we have seen in chapter 1.

Something is happening; it's just not solid and truly existent. We still have vivid experiences. We are not totally delusional. Well, maybe we are delusional from this point of view, but our delusions are based on some arising of experience. Emptiness is quite fertile: all thoughts, energy, and perceptions arise out of the womb of emptiness. Whatever occurs is not solid and real, yet something still happens. This has always felt like a bit of magic to me: even though we cannot find anything real, still a kind of brilliance keeps occurring. Then, in turn, these vivid experiences dissolve once again into emptiness.

If we look closely at anything, we can penetrate into both its empty and its vibrant nature. A common example is to look at a flower. I have a friend who grows outrageous dahlias in her garden. From the point of view of emptiness, there is nothing solid in any particular dahlia. It is clearly impermanent and will wither and die with the first frost, if not sooner. It has no true unchanging color or shape. It begins little and grows larger. It is made up of the rays of the sun, the compost in the soil, the water, the bulb from which it emerged. It is made up even of my friend's hard work, her breakfast, the tools she uses, and myriad other things. When we look into each of these, they, too, are the result of interdependence. There is nothing solid to be found. They are empty not only of our thoughts about them but of any unchanging, independent existence. Still, there is a big, showy dahlia to enjoy.

In 1992, I had the good fortune to have an interview with Khenpo Tsültrim Gyamtso Rinpoche, a senior teacher in the Kagyu lineage of Tibetan Buddhism. I wanted to meet with him because he had written a wonderful small book on emptiness.[1] I was thinking of using it with my students, but I hesitated because my personal understanding of emptiness was certainly more intellectual than experiential. I had the opportunity to ask him about teaching emptiness. He said two things that have stuck with me. First, he said it was all right for me to use his book as long as I continued my own meditation practice. Not only would my practice give me the opportunity to recognize the direct experience of emptiness, but it could also remind me that my ideas about emptiness are not the same as emptiness itself. And second, he said that in teaching about emptiness it was essential, always, to first make sure that my students and I understood the truth of suffering. It is all too easy to mistake an intellectual understanding of emptiness as a way of thinking we can bypass the direct experience of suffering and pain. John Welwood coined the term "spiritual bypassing" for this attempt to escape the pain of personal emotions or interpersonal relationships through the misuse of spiritual teachings.[2] As we saw in chapter 3, trying to evade pain is a cause of suffering, not a solution to it. This is an important reminder for everyone who studies emptiness, and it is especially crucial for therapists.

EMPTINESS IN THE THERAPEUTIC ENCOUNTER

An understanding of emptiness has implications for how we approach our work as therapists. It can alter how we listen to our clients as well as how we regard our own favorite theories of what might be happening in therapy.

Holding the Story Lightly

As therapists, if we remember this advice from Khenpo Tsültrim Gyamtso Rinpoche, we can simultaneously recognize both how painful suffering is while at the same time seeing that it is empty of any true existence. What does that mean? To begin with, generally it means that it is not helpful to our clients when we collude with them so that they need not experience anything painful in therapy. Nor do we avoid the sharpness of being with our clients' pain ourselves. Instead, we invite our clients (and ourselves) to bring curiosity and mindfulness to what they are actually experiencing. In that way we follow the Khenpo's advice to acknowledge the truth of suffering. Of course, there will be times that we help our clients establish some stability in their lives before tackling their more difficult experiences, but the ultimate goal is to assist our clients in taking a path toward working with their experience of suffering. At the same time, we can hold lightly the story line that a client brings to us. Not only do we understand that the story is the result of many causes and conditions coming together, but we also understand that these causes and conditions are themselves not solid and real.

Recognizing the Emptiness of Projections and Diagnostic Labels

Therapists and counselors are actually quite well-trained in recognizing that both our clients' and our own versions of things may be riddled with projection, transference, and countertransference. Where Buddhism goes further is in seeing that there is no absolute truth to be found even when we have thoroughly examined these projections. Story lines are just that: stories with varying degrees of accuracy but never completely true.

Emptiness implies that any time we use a label or diagnosis to describe a client's situation, we could remember that it is only a label, another story. It is not unusual to forget that a diagnosis is a convenient description. Sometimes therapists start to call clients by their diagnoses as though that is who they were: "a borderline," "a psychotic." Whenever we do this, we are turning diagnosis into a kind of ego, a false sense of a person, which inevitably leaves out the uniqueness and the ever-changing process of who that person is.

Being Willing Not to Know

An essential feature of our experience as therapists is uncertainty, not knowing. Alternatively, putting this in Buddhist terms, we could say that we as therapists need to learn to be able to rest in emptiness or openness. When we embrace and understand emptiness, we will be more able confidently to experience whatever arises when we are with our clients, be it more confusion or flashes of wisdom. Otherwise, we are just as likely to help our clients come up with yet another false story.

Having said that, I would also like to say that some stories and thoughts are more constructive than others. Sometimes, our work is to assist clients in finding more useful narratives. Cognitive-behavioral therapy and its variations can be quite helpful in showing clients how their thoughts lead to feelings and behavior. Replacing dysfunctional thoughts and habitual patterns with more encouraging ones can be enormously useful. Still, we can understand that these thoughts are what the Buddhists call "skillful means," and they are not ultimately true.

Supporting Clients' Discoveries of Emptiness

When we have an understanding of emptiness, we may hear what our clients say in a new way. I worked with a young man recently who confessed to me that he had always had a sense of things not feeling really solid. Carl even called this feeling "emptiness." When he had shared this feeling some years previously with his pastor, the clergyman had told Carl that he was depressed and needed medication. "I know I'm not depressed," he told me. "I just know that all the things I've tried to be aren't really who I am."

He went on to list the different ego-stories he had tried unsuccessfully to maintain: high school football player, mechanic, guitar-playing folk singer, graduate student, father, husband. While he had done all of these things, none of them felt satisfyingly "real" to him. He experienced tenderness and longing as he described this to me, but he was not depressed. From a Buddhist point of view, he was recognizing egolessness and emptiness.

Often what we as therapists are trying to do is help our clients find ways of being that are more spontaneous, creative, open-minded, and flexible. We would like them to let go of their fixed ideas about themselves, their partners, and their lives. They would like to feel more connected with themselves and others. These therapy goals are, in fact, also "emptiness" goals.

One last implication of emptiness for therapists is recognizing that our role, and even the practice of psychotherapy altogether, is empty. It is tempting to identify ourselves as some kind of helper and make a story about ourselves based on it. To the extent that we solidify such a view, we then require someone to need our help. We end up with a dualistic predicament: for me to be a helper, I need someone to help. This can lead to codependence (not to be confused with interdependence). Codependence is ego based, not emptiness based. In order to feel important or special or even just "existent," I may cling to my identity as "psychologist" or "psychotherapist" or "counselor" or whatever label I have assumed.

We can easily make a big deal out of therapy. Instead, we could see that it is simply an available form. Because there is such a thing in the culture as "therapy," we can take that empty form and possibly be of help to people who are suffering.

7

may i be a bridge,
a ship, or a ... psychotherapist?

an introduction to contemplative psychotherapy

SOME PRACTITIONERS of Mahayana Buddhism choose to take the bodhisattva vow, introduced in chapter 1. In that vow, they state their willingness to be whatever beings might need: a bridge, a ship, a doctor, some medicine. The wording of that eighth-century vow doesn't mention psychotherapy, but like aspiring bodhisattvas, professional therapists have the desire to benefit beings—in this case, their clients—by relieving their suffering and helping them connect with their inherent wisdom and compassion. In this chapter we will look at the orientation of contemplative psychotherapy, an approach that is based on the Buddhist principles we have been considering.

THE VIEW OF BRILLIANT SANITY

The root concept that informs the field of contemplative psychotherapy is "brilliant sanity," a term coined by Chögyam Trungpa Rinpoche for his students who worked in the field of psychology.[1] "Brilliant sanity" refers to the inherent, natural qualities of the mind, which are identified as spaciousness, clarity, and compassion.

Spaciousness

Spaciousness refers to the emptiness quality of mind. As we have seen, there is nothing solid and unchanging in the mind. Instead, we could imagine it as a limitless, open space. Into that space, experiences arise: thoughts, emotions, images, perceptions, and sensations. A common image for this aspect of mind and brilliant sanity is the sky. The vast sky does not reject anything that comes into it: fluffy white summer clouds, dark thunderstorms, birds, planes, even pollution. In the same way, our minds have the capacity to accommodate any experience without rejecting it or pushing it away. This quality is also called "openness": the mind can accommodate any experience.

Perhaps it would be useful to note that "mind," in the Buddhist sense, is not the same as "brain." Sometimes "mind" refers to the dualistic mind of ego. Another aspect of mind is the "sixth sense," which is described below. "Mind" is also used to refer to what we are calling brilliant sanity: the awakened "mind" of bodhichitta, our inherent nature itself.

Clarity

The quality of clarity refers to the wisdom of mind that recognizes all experiences with precision and allows us to connect fully with anything that arises in our experience. In the Buddhist tradition, in addition to the ordinary five senses with which we are all familiar, there is considered to be a sixth sense that allows us to be mindful and aware of the activities of mind: thoughts, memories, fantasies, images, and so on. Clarity is the quality of mind that does not flinch but instead simply sees, hears, smells, tastes, touches, and "minds" all aspects of our experience without distortion. This is not to imply that brilliant sanity involves our senses becoming more acute than they actually are. As I am growing older, for example, I am noticing that my hearing is not as sharp as it once was. Clarity means that I hear however I actually hear at this point, not according to some external standard. Another word used for the clarity aspect of brilliant sanity is "awareness." We can bring our awareness to any experience at all.

Often these first two qualities of brilliant sanity are described as inseparable. Awareness and openness—or put another way, wisdom and emptiness—are a single thing, not two separate things: the vast openness of mind is imbued with awareness itself. Compassion, the third quality of brilliant sanity, is sometimes described as arising out of inseparable emptiness and wisdom. As we have seen in the discussion of bodhichitta, the desire to alleviate suffering is simply an aspect of who we are as sentient beings, and it is what leads us to become counselors and psychotherapists. Although we describe the qualities of brilliant sanity one by one, they are not actually separate. Instead, they are all aspects of our nonconceptual nature.

The Unconditionality of Brilliant Sanity

From the point of view of brilliant sanity, not only are these three qualities of mind inherent, they are unconditional. They are present in us even when we are not aware of them. No matter what our state of mind or situation in life, these qualities are our true nature. There are no conditions required for us to have brilliant sanity. It is just how things are. As we saw with the woman who worried about the children, even in psychotic states of mind, these qualities may be expressed, albeit with an overlay of confusion.

They are present in all of us: therapists, clients, relatives, friends, and enemies. Yes, even terrorists and perpetrators of violence are understood to have this inherent nature. Clearly, though, we are not always in touch with these qualities in ourselves. As contemplative psychotherapists, our aspiration is to help clients connect, or reconnect, with their brilliant sanity.

BEGINNING WITH OURSELVES

Like Buddhism, contemplative psychotherapy teaches that we begin with ourselves. The view of contemplative psychotherapy is that we cannot nurture and support our clients' brilliant sanity if we are not familiar with our own. As we have seen, confusion is quite powerful and often subtle as well. It is easy to mistakenly substitute our ideas of brilliant sanity for the genuine experience.

In working with a client, I may think to myself that what he needs is a greater sense of compassion for himself. I may try various things to bring that about. They might be fine ideas, but they are not the actual experience of brilliant sanity. I may even feel a sense of compassion for the client, myself. To the extent that I have a sense of myself as separate from my client and a sense of my compassion somehow going from me to him in a dualistic way, this is not a glimpse of brilliant sanity, either. A true experience of brilliant sanity would not contain the self-consciousness of ego.

I'm always a bit wary of describing an experience and saying that it was one of brilliant sanity. Still, let me offer this example of what may have been a glimpse of it. I was staying in a cabin in the mountains when I chanced to look out through the screen door and saw a brown bear. She was standing on her hind legs and looking back at me. I noticed that there were yellow tags in both of her ears and I was aware of the grunting sound that she was making. I noted that the door was flimsy. The thought arose to make a noise and scare her away. "Yaaaah!" I yelled. She dropped to all fours, turned around, and ambled away.

In the time that we looked at each other, I didn't have any particular sense of self-consciousness. I was simply present. The thoughts that arose were practical and in the moment. There was a timeless and open quality to the whole encounter. Was that brilliant sanity? Once I ask the question, I am already in a different sort of experience, one that is evaluating and reflecting, rather than one of nondual presence.

In the contemplative approach, we work with ourselves through the sitting practice of mindfulness-awareness meditation, introduced in the next chapter. Through our ongoing sitting practice, we become intimately familiar with our own minds in both clarity and confusion. We come to know our own personal styles of leaving the present moment and of getting caught up in passion, aggression, and ignorance.

Meditation practice provides a powerful antidote to the story lines of ego. We become expert in recognizing when we are hanging on to both overt and subtle versions of ourselves. In addition, we also come to see how we re-create story lines as a way of pulling back from the very experiences we long for: spaciousness, clarity, and compassion. We may discover how we turn away from the vastness of spaciousness. We may want to avoid feeling groundless and uncertain. So too with clarity: we may prefer to have a softer edge on reality when experiences arise that disconfirm our favorite ego-story lines. We may subtly rework memories rather than see ourselves in an embarrassing or shameful light. We also may shrink away from our naturally tender and compassionate nature when to stay present means feeling our own pain or recognizing the pain of others. Instead, we may wince and turn away when we see another suffering.

It is not uncommon to find we don't have time to visit a friend who is ill or who is going through a divorce. We intend to go or call, yet somehow we don't get there. Maybe we send an e-mail or leave a voice message. "I don't want to intrude," we tell ourselves. In fact, I told myself that this very morning. I have a friend whose father is in intensive care. I thought I would leave a voice-mail message on her office phone. Then, you see, I wouldn't be pestering her at home at a difficult time. I also wouldn't be offering much support, either. As I ask myself now what I am avoiding, I find that I don't want to feel helpless. I don't want to feel sad or even frightened, perhaps, by the reality of her father's possible death. It may bring up painful memories of my own father's death. It may remind me that my own mother was in the hospital overnight just last week. There is plenty of uncertainty in my own life—can't I avoid inviting hers, too?

It is not that we are coldhearted or bad friends. It is actually the opposite. We *are* tenderhearted; we do connect with others' pain. Having written this, I realized that I didn't need to hold back, and I just called my friend. Her father is out of danger, but it has been a frightening few days. We were both touched by connecting with each other now, when the reality of death is so very much in the air.

Sometimes, as when we avoid another's (and our own) pain, we are shrinking from intensity. Other times, we are steering clear of spaciousness. As we come to see our internal narratives for what they are, stories that distance us from our direct experience, they begin to lose their power. We may find that nothing much is happening, and we may come up with a new story, "I'm bored" or even, "I'm boring." As we allow ourselves to just experience this so-called boredom, we may find that we can simply rest in the spacious aspect of brilliant sanity.

My client David worked as a computer engineer. He was often very busy and spent a good deal of his time thinking—"in my head," he would say. In our work together, sometimes he would begin to feel bored. Like many Americans, he had internalized the idea that feeling boredom was somehow wrong. It meant that he was uninteresting or that he didn't know what to do. Boredom and uncertainty were linked. Together we began to explore what happened when he simply experienced his boredom or uncertainty instead of trying to escape from them. For David, it led to a decrease in anxiety. An unexpected benefit was that allowing himself not to know what to do next led to a kind of freedom in meeting new people. If he didn't have to escape from not knowing or from boredom, he could simply show up with others and see what happened.

THE THERAPEUTIC RELATIONSHIP

In contemplative psychotherapy, the vehicle both for working with ego and for recognizing brilliant sanity is the therapeutic relationship itself. Let's note some of the key aspects of such a relationship.

Genuineness

First, the therapeutic relationship is "genuine," which means, for me, that it is not based on ego. As a contemplative psychotherapist, my work is informed by my mindfulness-awareness meditation practice. As I sit with clients, my practice is to again and again let go of my stories about myself and about my clients. The main thing that I am offering is my full presence, my willingness to be with whatever arises. Only on the basis of being present with my direct experience, as much as possible, can I respond to my client in a skillful way.

A genuine relationship is one in which both parties are present with their direct experience. Obviously, our clients do not arrive already able to do this. In fact, we ourselves are only able to do this some of the time. Still, in contemplative psychotherapy, that is our aspiration and our reference point. A useful technique that is introduced in the next chapter, "touch and go," helps us to keep returning to our direct experience in the moment.

From both the Buddhist and contemplative points of view, the biggest obstacle to experiencing our inherent brilliant sanity, or even our ordinary day-to-day functionality, is the attempt to maintain ego. As we noted in earlier chapters, the attempt to maintain a solid and fixed sense of self leads to a stagnant way of being. When we seek refuge in certainty, in fixed roles or "expertise," we cut ourselves off from the freshness, spontaneity, and creativity of brilliant sanity. A genuine relationship challenges this attempt to maintain a separate, permanent, and solid sense of ourselves in a number of ways.

Exchange

By actually connecting with another person, the illusion of separateness becomes undermined. My peer consultant and I often note, as we present our work to each other, how often it is our own attempts to be separate from our clients that is keeping us from being as helpful to our clients as we could be. Getting caught up in analyzing transferences, countertransferences, or resistances can become ways of not being present. It is not that these things have no importance; it is that we can easily misuse them as ways of distancing ourselves from what is happening in the moment.

What I am feeling as I sit with my client is affected by what my client is experiencing. And for my client, what he or she experiences is also influenced by what I am experiencing. In contemplative psychotherapy, we call our direct experience of another "exchange." Exchange happens because we are not separate but, instead, are interconnected, interdependent. As I talk to my friend on the phone about her father, for example, I pick up on her sadness. I, too, feel sad, not only in reaction but through our direct connection. For a moment we may glimpse the nonduality of our experience.

The experience we call "exchange" is not what we imagine is going on for our client; it is our actual felt experience in the presence of the client. Like all experiences, from a Buddhist point of view, it is filtered through our habitual patterns—still, exchange provides us with a wealth of information if we attend to it. Through our meditation practice, through our consultation and supervision with other professionals, and through talking with our clients, we can often identify the source of a particular experience as exchange. Often, we don't actually know, so we always hold lightly the conclusion that the source of an experience is exchange. Once we have an experience, whether its source is exchange or not, it is ours now to work with as we would with any experience.

Let me offer a brief example to clarify a bit. Josh is a large young man. He is telling me about a situation in which he felt quite frightened of another man, Jack, who was threatening to hurt him. As I sit with Josh, I notice that I am shrinking back from him. I am trembling a little, and I am thinking that he is sitting between me and the door. I am wondering what would happen if he got mad at me. I am feeling scared.

A number of different things could be going on. First, as a small woman, to the extent that I may have my own issues about large men who I perceive as threatening, my fear is based on countertransference. I may also simply feel afraid because Josh might, in fact, be moving toward doing something dangerous. This could simply be an accurate response in the moment. Finally, my fear of being threatened may be exchange with Josh. As he tells me this story, he may be feeling fear similar to what he felt with Jack. My perception of Josh as threatening may arise from Josh's own sense of feeling threatened. If I am not aware of the possibility of exchange, I may easily mistake my fear as evidence that I am with a frightening man instead of a frightened one.

Sometimes therapists identify clients as "difficult," when what may be going on is a particularly painful experience of exchange. I suspect that some clients who are labeled "borderline" may be like this for many of us.

When it is difficult to stay present with the exchange, we may distance ourselves from our clients without even realizing it. In chapter 20, we will look at the practice of "body-speech-mind" as a way of identifying and letting go of obstacles that prevent us from being present with exchange.

From the point of view of egolessness, what is happening in any moment is an ever-changing dance. Both we and our clients are continually changing. I am not who I was last week and neither is my client. In fact, we are not exactly who we were even a moment ago. "Picking up where we left off last week," loses meaning in such a view. Recognizing how each of us, and also the relationship itself, are continually changing highlights the truth of impermanence.

Trying to find "who we really are," some essential core self, is an exercise in futility from the point of view of egolessness. A genuine relationship reveals the lack of solidity in its participants. Instead, it supports the curiosity, courage, and warmth it takes to live authentically. This implies, too, that as therapists it is not helpful to take on a fixed role, one designed to protect a false sense of ourselves. This does not mean that we reveal everything that arises in our mind or blurt out opinions and judgments in the interest of being "genuine." It means that when we show up, we actually show up. We are present with our own experience, with our confusion and our wisdom. We speak from the ground of being present even when, or maybe especially when, we are not sure of ourselves.

RECOGNIZING BRILLIANT SANITY

A final principle of contemplative psychotherapy is its emphasis on recognizing and nurturing inherent sanity. It is much easier to describe confusion. We have manuals that provide us with categories and subcategories of the many varieties of confusion and mental disorder. Since, from the Buddhist point of view, we all tend to avoid uncertainty, not knowing, and pain, it is easy to understand how we might choose to become expert in the things that we *can* readily know and describe. Falling into labeling and being attached to those labels is one of the ways that our avoidance of emptiness may manifest.

Since brilliant sanity is a nonconceptual experience, it is challenging to describe and recognize its signs. Still, there are some hallmarks that point us toward the experiences of brilliant sanity in ourselves and in our clients. The first things are simply recognizing the qualities of spaciousness, clarity, and compassion in ourselves and in those with whom we work. We have already looked a bit at that. In addition, we can say that we are glimpsing brilliant sanity when we encounter positive qualities that reflect our inherent wisdom and compassion, such as loving-kindness, compassion, joy, and equanimity (the "four immeasurables," which will be examined in greater detail in part 2 of this book), as well as generosity, discipline, patience, exertion, mindfulness, and wisdom (the "six awakened actions," which will be explained in part 3).

Some other signposts of brilliant sanity include the experiences of revulsion and doubt.

Framing our discussion in the context of the Buddhist tradition, for instance, we would say that revulsion with samsara, the world of confusion perpetuated by ego-grasping, is one of the main motivations leading a person to a spiritual path. Similarly, clients often seek out therapy when they are revolted by their habitual patterns. They may say something like "I'm just sick of this" or "I'm completely fed up." Underneath such dissatisfaction, or even self-aggression, lies a clarity that glimpses the possibility of what we have called the Third Noble Truth: the possibility of the cessation of suffering.

Doubt is another important sign of brilliant sanity, because it is a reflection of uncertainty, openness. A client who says, "I'm not sure if this job is good for me," is opening up his mind. He may be ready to look more deeply into his habitual avoidance of personal challenge. For the contemplative psychotherapist, becoming curious about the direct experience of doubt itself may be useful as well.

Similarly, when clients experience a gap in their story lines, instead of rushing in and saying, "You were talking about your mother," I may ask something like, "What is it like to suddenly find yourself here, not knowing what you were talking about?" Sometimes clients ignore that kind of question and go right back into their original or another story. Other times clients become interested in the direct experience of not knowing. Being able to tolerate uncertainty is a valuable skill.

I have my own three favorite signs of brilliant sanity, which my students like to tease me about. The first is awkwardness, which often serves as the sign that a person is not caught up in a habitual pattern. Not knowing what to do in a particular setting or social situation can mean that instead of relying on a familiar role learned in one's family of origin, for example, one is simply present and available in the moment. As we saw with my engineer client, David, the willingness to feel awkward and uncertain can be socially liberating.

Second, "corniness," or even sentimentality, can be an indication of the willingness to feel pain or it can be an expression of compassion. With a bit of embarrassment, a client named Judy told me about crying at a "silly romantic movie." As we explored what had touched her heart, it became apparent that the heroine of the film had a relationship with her father like the one Judy had always longed for, but never had, with her own father. That longing was present in the moment as we talked about it together. We experienced a sense of connection with each other as she let herself feel her own sense of sorrow.

Finally among my personal favorites is "stupidity," as the label we might put on the experience of not knowing. Many of us who become therapists come from backgrounds in which "being smart" is highly valued. Certainly in my own high school and college experience, saying "I don't know" was to be avoided at all costs. To "not know" was the same as being stupid. I have found it personally freeing to go toward the direct experience of stupidity rather than trying to cover it up. What I have found is that "feeling stupid" is often just the experience of spaciousness, one of the key elements of brilliant sanity.

Having the view of brilliant sanity encourages us to allow clarity to arise out of emptiness. Not already knowing what to do is the best foundation for creative, compassionate, and truly responsive clinical work.

Part Two
connecting with the heart
of a bodhisattva

May all sentient beings enjoy happiness
and the root of happiness.
May they be free from suffering and the root of suffering.
May they not be separated from the great
happiness devoid of suffering.
May they dwell in the great equanimity free from
passion, aggression, and prejudice.

—*The Four Limitless Ones Chant*

8
meditation
the practice of connecting with ourselves

IN THERAPY, our first task is usually establishing rapport, making a connection with our client. Without finding some human link with each other, therapist and client can't have a genuine relationship. We actually lay the foundation for such relationships, however, by beginning with ourselves.

In contemplative psychotherapy, the main way we connect with ourselves is through the sitting practice of mindfulness-awareness meditation. This chapter presents basic instruction in a particular practice of mindfulness-awareness meditation that is especially relevant for counselors and psychotherapists.

MINDFULNESS AND AWARENESS

Some varieties of meditation practice are designed to help the practitioner relax; others are meant to produce an altered state of mind. Some use elaborate visualizations; others have hardly any technique at all. Some require the meditator not to move while others, like tai chi, are moving meditation practices. These practices differ because they are based on different intentions. The practice we are introducing here is a mindfulness-awareness practice.

Instead of helping us to attain a different state of mind or body, this type of meditation aims at fostering aspects of our being that are already present within us: mindfulness and awareness. Although the term *mindfulness* is used in different ways by different writers, what we mean by the term here is precise, moment-to-moment attention to the details of experience. Mindfulness has been receiving a good deal of attention lately in counseling and psychotherapy articles and books. I have seen it discussed as a method of working with depression, anxiety, pain management, and eating disorders, among others. But really, mindfulness has always been a part of psychotherapy. We direct our clients to bring precise attention to something: the free flow of associations, dreams, the number of times a particular behavior is repeated and leads to a particular reward, the content of thoughts and emotions, and so on. In this sense, there is nothing new about mindfulness. It is an essential part of any approach we might want to take in working with the mind.

In the meditation practice we are introducing here, we are interested in cultivating unconditional mindfulness. That is, rather than choosing to be mindful of a particular aspect of our experience, we want to become mindful of whatever arises. We are interested in cultivating the clarity and open-ended curiosity that is part of our brilliant sanity. Moreover, we are interested in developing awareness. Like mindfulness, awareness is an aspect of brilliant sanity. While mindfulness directs us to the details of our experience, awareness refers to the larger context, the space within which experience arises. In this sense, it is closely related to spaciousness and emptiness.

The following example may help to clarify the difference between mindfulness and awareness. I recently attended a professional conference that ended, on the last evening, with a celebratory dance. People were crowded together out on the floor, dancing to the music of a live band. At one point I was dancing with a man who was leading me in a tango, and both mindfulness and awareness were necessary to negotiate our way: attending to the details of that particular dance form required mindfulness, and moving across the floor without running into other dancers required awareness.

Mindfulness-awareness meditation practice gives us the opportunity to recognize both of these interdependent aspects of our inherent nature. We begin with the development of mindfulness, which lets the mind settle down a bit with itself. The idea isn't to get our minds to do something new or unusual. Rather, we are letting the mind simply rest. The Sanskrit term *shamatha,* which means "abiding in peace," is the Buddhist term for this kind of practice, in which we place our attention on one object, for example, the breath. Yet the peace we are seeking to cultivate may not be all that placid. Instead, we practice abiding with whatever comes up in our experience. That could include tranquillity, but it could just as easily be moments of anxiety, anger, or sadness.

I started my own meditation practice when my best friend from high school unexpectedly died at the age of thirty-two. For the first time in my life, I experienced bouts of intense anxiety. My heart raced, my palms became sweaty, strong fear arose, and my usual distractions were no help. I churned out thoughts about how this feeling would never go away and that I was probably going to die any moment now. A close friend suggested that I try meditating. I had already done some reading about meditation and attended some talks about it, so I was receptive to his suggestion.

What I found was that I could simply sit with my experience. Instead of adding a layer of panic about how I would never stop feeling this awful, my sitting practice let me be present moment by moment with the waves of shakiness, thoughts of death, and physical signs of fear. I stopped scaring myself about being anxious. The more I sat, the more I could see how I had been making myself feel even worse. I began to relax with myself, and there was a quality of unconditional peace in that, even though waves of strong discomfort continued to arise and fall away.

In sitting practice we use a simple technique that shows us when we have wandered off from being simply present. As the mind begins to settle down with the precision of the technique, it naturally begins to recognize its awareness nature as well. In that way, mindfulness practice becomes mindfulness-awareness practice. Shamatha practice opens out into what is known in Buddhism as *shamatha-vipashyana* practice. The Sanskrit word *vipashyana* is usually translated as "insight," and it is characterized by the spacious quality of brilliant sanity, what is sometimes called "panoramic awareness." So, this practice, which in this book we will simply refer to as mindfulness-awareness meditation, cultivates awareness without losing the precision of mindfulness.

MINDFULNESS-AWARENESS
MEDITATION PRACTICE: GUIDED EXERCISE

What follows is a description of the technique of mindfulness-awareness meditation practice. I suggest that you read all of the instructions before you begin, and then you can try it out. Then, after you've given it a try, you might want to read the instructions again to see if you find the answers to any questions that may have arisen once you have actually done it. (Generally, by the way, it is best to receive meditation instruction from a trained meditation instructor, not from words in a book. For those who would like to go further with a meditation practice, information about centers that provide meditation instruction are listed in the Resources section at the end of this book.)

Since what we are trying to do is to be with ourselves as we already are, this technique is fairly simple. It is not particularly easy, because it goes against our habitual patterns to just sit down with ourselves, but it is simple. There are three main aspects to the technique: posture, breath, and thoughts.

Posture

We begin by finding a good seat. It is traditional to sit down on the floor. There are a variety of sitting cushions and benches that people use, and all of them are designed to help the practitioner sit up straight with as little discomfort as possible. Sometimes people fold up a blanket to sit on. It is also fine to sit on a chair. Basically, we want the back to be strong and erect and the front of the body to be relaxed and open. Also, whatever seat we choose, we want it to be stable and not wiggling around.

Once we've chosen our seat, we sit down and cross our legs in front of us. It is not necessary, or even recommended with this practice, to fold one's legs into a full or half lotus. Just cross the legs in front as you may have done as a child. You will probably find that you are more comfortable if your hips are higher than your knees. Adding a folded blanket to your cushion or chair may help you achieve that. If you sit in a chair, put your feet flat on the floor, perhaps placing something under your feet so they can rest flat comfortably.

Then, let your spine rise up from that good seat. The lower back has a natural curve in it, and we let that be. We place the hands, palms down, on top of our thighs or knees. Shoulders are squared to the front. The head is upright, not tilted downward. The chin gets tucked in just a little bit so that we are not straining the neck or looking upward. The jaw is relaxed; it may be helpful to let the mouth open a little bit.

The eyes are open. This is a key point for this practice. One of the reasons we teach this practice to counselors and therapists is that it helps us to be present not only with ourselves but also with others. Having the eyes open supports our ability to bring the mindfulness and awareness that we cultivate "on the cushion" into our relationships off the cushion.

We place our gaze on the floor in front of us, about four to six feet away. Whatever is in front of us—in a meditation program it might be someone else's back—we just let it be there. The gaze can be focused or "soft." If we focus too intently, we may find that we develop a stiff neck or even a headache.

So, to review the posture: take a good, solid seat with a strong back and an open front. Rest the hands on the top of the legs. Let the head and shoulders be upright, with the chin slightly tucked in. Rest your gaze in front of you and down. The posture is dignified and upright but not unnatural.

You might try sitting just like this, in this posture, without doing anything more, for a few minutes. When your mind wanders, simply come back to sitting in this posture.

Breath

Next, we add working with the breath. Since we are interested in being unconditionally present with whatever arises, we do not manipulate the breath at all. We just let it be however it is: deep, shallow, fast, slow. It doesn't matter. We pay attention primarily to the out-breath. As the breath goes out, we place our attention on it. As it dissolves into space, the attention we have placed on it dissolves as well. Then, the in-breath happens naturally, and there is no special technique associated with it. As you might already see, this practice gives us the opportunity, again and again, to let go with the out-breath. Or, we might say, "going out with the out-breath" is already letting go, and the practice lets us notice it. This highlighting of letting go is another reason this particular practice is a relevant one for therapists and counselors, since our own and our clients' suffering and confusion are caused by grasping and holding on to mistaken ideas.

Again, you might try just these first two parts of the practice for a few minutes: sitting with the posture and being with the breath.

Thoughts

Finally, the third aspect of the technique is relating with thoughts. It will soon become apparent as we practice meditation that we readily get caught up in our thoughts and forget where we are and what we are doing. Once we notice that we have been caught up—that is to say, once we are aware of where we are again—we acknowledge that we were "gone," by using a silent, mental label. "Thinking," we say to ourselves. In terms of this mindfulness-awareness practice, we regard anything that takes us away from simply sitting with the posture and going out with the out-breath as "thinking." It is generally most useful to limit our use of the label for when we are actually caught up and forget what we're doing. Don't bother using it for brief thoughts that come and go but are not big distractions.

I think of using this label as akin to a weather report: "Thinking has just occurred here." It is not, "You idiot, you were lost in thought." It's not even, "Thinking is wrong, I'm not really practicing." Thinking is one of the activities of the mind, and it is simply included in the practice. We are not trying to get ourselves to stop thinking. We are interested in seeing what is happening and who we are, not in seeing who we are if we impose a self-aggressive regimen on ourselves. This is often quite difficult to believe, and practitioners often find that they have begun to judge their practice based on how many times they become caught up in thoughts. That is a mistake.

While it is true that the more we practice, the more the activity of mind does indeed settle down, this settling will not happen by forcing ourselves to be any particular way. When we let ourselves simply be, then, paradoxically, we give ourselves the opportunity to recognize the natural qualities of mindfulness and awareness in ourselves.

A traditional metaphor often used to describe meditation practice is giving a big roomy meadow to a wild horse. If we can take the attitude of giving ourselves enough room to see what we are doing, while also putting a fence around that big meadow with the technique itself, our wild-horse minds will become tame without losing their natural liveliness.

THE PRACTICE OF TOUCH AND GO

The ability to be present and to both touch experience and also to let it go are pivotal skills in the practice of counseling and psychotherapy. They are cultivated in this mindfulness-awareness meditation practice through a technique that Chögyam Trungpa called "touch and go."[1] As we have already described, the basic technique of sitting meditation works with posture, breath, and thoughts. As we sit on our cushions, all kinds of experiences arise. As in my own first meditation experiences, intense emotions may arise. Lots of thoughts may come, or physical sensations may be present. Equally, nothing much may happen. The whole thing may feel boring. In any case, we use the technique known as "touch and go" to work further with the arising of any kind of experience. Touch and go is a way of momentarily connecting with our experience and then allowing it to dissolve again.

It is perhaps easier to describe touch and go by first describing what it is not. Some years ago I was working with a group of students at Sharpham College in Devon, England, and we came up with the following exercise. Begin by sitting on your meditation seat and conjuring up a juicy emotion or a vivid fantasy. Now, just keep it going. If you find yourself becoming mindful of the present moment, quickly return to being lost in distraction. Continue for at least five minutes. We called this "touch and grab," or even "touch and wallow." Notice what it feels like to you. There may be a sense of stuffiness or even claustrophobia. It may or may not feel familiar.

The next thing touch and go is not is "go and go." To practice this one, again settle yourself on your meditation seat. Now, whatever arises, do not get into it at all. Be like one of those water bugs that live on the surface tension of the water and hardly get their feet wet. At the mere hint of an experience, let it go. Again, continue this for around five minutes and then notice what you experience. Many people find that their minds get quite speedy and even aggressive.

Then, try touch and go. When an experience arises, gently touch or taste it. Then, allow it to go, or go along. Since all that arises is impermanent, each moment is already changing, it is already going. Let it. How long should you touch? I usually suggest to people that they think of how long it would take to recognize their favorite food if it were placed into their mouth while their eyes were closed. How long would it take to recognize chocolate? Or butter pecan ice cream? Or béarnaise sauce? It doesn't take too long. Touch about that long.

Another useful exercise for illustrating touch and go was introduced to me by Bob Wing, a Naropa martial arts instructor. He had a group of us wander around in a room, and his instruction to us was that when we met other people, we should shake their hands. On the first round of hand-shaking, we practiced "touch and grab," by gazing into each others' faces and clinging just a moment longer than was comfortable. We next tried "go and go," by barely touching others' hands and not looking at their faces. Finally, we practiced "touch and go," by shaking hands, looking at the other person's face, and then letting go. Many of the participants reported that they felt irritated and imposed upon by touch and grab, dismissed by go and go, and more relaxed with touch and go. Perhaps you could imagine what it would be like to do this exercise. Or, you could play with its basic ideas when you greet other people in your life.

STARTING A MEDITATION PRACTICE

If meditation is new to you, it is helpful to begin with short sessions. You might try fifteen or twenty minutes at a time. A daily practice is best. In the spirit of developing an unconditional attitude toward your experience, it would be good to have a regular time to sit and an already decided length of time before you start. If you fall into the habit of stopping your practice when it's difficult or keeping going when it is pleasant, you make your practice conditional and that undermines your purpose. As you become more familiar with what you are doing, you can extend the time. Many people sit for forty-five minutes to an hour, or more, daily.

Often people find it helpful to sit with a group. If that is available where you live, you might try that. Otherwise, sit on your own. Perhaps you may want to set up a particular spot in your home where you sit. When you practice with your eyes open, what's in front of you can matter. Needless to say, it is better to have something neutral or inspiring in front of you than something that will remind you of the many things you are not doing while you're sitting.

It is always fine to stop in the middle of a session and just begin again. Take a moment or two to look around the room and then start again. "Taking a fresh start" in this way can be helpful if you have become particularly confused or extremely drowsy. If your legs fall asleep or if your posture is painful, simply rearrange yourself. The idea is to have a friendly attitude without giving in to mere entertaining distraction.

In contemplative psychotherapy we say that you can do psychotherapy without a meditation practice, but you cannot do contemplative psychotherapy without one. As we have already seen, it is quite easy to substitute our thoughts for direct experience. By helping us return again and again to direct experience, a daily meditation practice keeps us honest.

SHOULD THERAPISTS TEACH THEIR CLIENTS TO MEDITATE?

If our sitting practice is so important for our own development, does this mean that we should teach our clients to meditate? From one point of view, it seems obvious that if meditation is such a useful practice, then we should certainly share it with our clients. It wouldn't be much of a stretch to see it as a violation of the teachings on compassion to withhold meditation instruction. Yet, for myself, I have come to a different conclusion about this issue.

Unlike psychotherapy, which most clients undertake for some limited time—even if it is a long time—meditation is a lifelong practice. I have to acknowledge that I would probably be very pleased if a client told me that he or she had begun to meditate. In fact, I'd be delighted if everyone began meditating. In my own experience, there is nothing else quite so powerful or persistent for wearing away confusion. However, if we introduce meditation practice to our clients, then it becomes a part of our psychotherapeutic relationship. This brings some problems.

It is important that our clients be free to feel any way at all toward us. They need to be able to reject us and any advice we may offer. I have some concern that, if I were to suggest that they meditate, my clients' meditation practices could become contingent on how they were feeling toward me. I would not want to interfere with their developing an ongoing practice in this way. Meditation is difficult enough without clients attaching it to their perception of my approval or disapproval of it.

Another issue is that most therapists are not also trained meditation instructors. For those therapists, there is an ethical issue involved, of not being qualified to teach meditation. Despite their good intentions, those not trained in how to teach meditation could mislead their clients both in their understanding of what meditation is and can do as well as in how to apply the technique as their practice unfolds.

Many of my clients know of my connection to Naropa University, so it is not unusual for them to ask me about meditation. I am a trained meditation instructor, but when clients express an interest in beginning a meditation practice, I refer them to a variety of other places in the community where they can learn to meditate. I make it a point to tell them of different traditions that are available locally, including sitting practices as well as contemplative movement practices like yoga and tai chi. If they then choose to discuss their experience of practice with me, I treat it as I would any other experience they choose to bring up. Since I do also work with meditation students in other settings, I take care not to impose my ideas about meditation practice on my clients' experiences of their own contemplative practices.

For some clients, having their therapist recommend meditation could lead to a mistaken understanding of what meditation is. As we have seen, it is not a method for changing or "curing" oneself. It is the simple practice of being unconditionally present with all that we are and allowing ourselves to discover both our confusion and our inherent awakened qualities. I saw a man for an initial consultation who had been meditating for more than twenty years in the hope that meditation would cut his painful obsessive thought process. It had not. He was still plagued by nearly constant violent sexual thoughts. He mistakenly believed that the presence of these thoughts was evidence of his being a poor meditation practitioner. In fact, the mindfulness that he had developed in his meditation practice had helped him recognize these thoughts as thoughts and had helped him not to take action based on any of them. Still, he needed a different kind of additional help. I referred him to a colleague for a psychiatric evaluation. He began to take medication, which gave him substantial relief from whatever chemical imbalance was producing his obsessive thoughts in the first place. This example illustrates that meditation is not a substitute for necessary psychotherapy or medical care.

A final point for me is that in the tradition in which I am trained, providing meditation instruction is part of my own Mahayana practice. I am either not paid for it or given a token amount of compensation. Certainly, it is a lot less expensive for my students to have me as their meditation instructor than it would be to have me as their therapist. For me to do both would create a dual relationship that is best avoided for economic, ethical, and therapeutic reasons.

Instead of teaching my clients to practice meditation, I help them develop mindfulness and awareness by applying the basic principles of meditation practice to their experience (as we will explore in chapter 19).

9

the first immeasurable

loving-kindness

As we discussed in depth at the beginning of this book, bodhichitta, or awakened heart, is at the core of our being. Everyone has tenderness toward someone or something: our parents, our children, our lovers, our dogs and cats, our favorite books, or our favorite foods. When that tenderness appears as the wish to benefit all other beings, it is called "aspiration bodhichitta."

A traditional method for arousing aspiration bodhichitta is to contemplate ways of relating to others that go beyond the habitual self-interest of ego-clinging. In Buddhism, there are four such ways of relating, which are called the four immeasurables, or the four limitless ones. They are (1) loving-kindness, (2) compassion, (3) joy, and (4) equanimity. Contemplating each of the four immeasurables helps us tune in to qualities that we already have, aspects of our natural wisdom, our awakened hearts. Doing the practice associated with the four immeasurables can help us reconnect with our deep longings to benefit others and also help us to recognize and support these yearnings in our clients.

Each of the four immeasurables is a natural quality of awakened heart or mind. When we engage in contemplating these four "limitless ones," we are uncovering qualities that are inherent in us, not trying to add qualities that we lack. They are called "limitless" because they are not constrained by the limits of a nonexistent ego; they are aspects of the boundless mind of the bodhisattva.

Unlike the rest of us who filter our experiences through ego and its stories and expectations about how things are, the mind of a fully awakened bodhisattva is beyond concept or measure. Our own minds, too, are fundamentally boundless, but we usually restrict our experience of our own limitless brilliant sanity with our habit of clinging to ego, and so fail to recognize our inherent nature.

In general, the expectation in Buddhist practice is that we would first tame or stabilize our minds through mindfulness-awareness meditation and only then turn to contemplations like those on the four immeasurables. I have found, though, for many of us, that working even at the outset of our meditation practice with contemplation on one or more of the four immeasurables can also bring stability to our minds while at the same time touching our hearts. You can explore for yourself which practices speak to you personally and decide in what order you would like to undertake them. In any case, this is the first of four chapters that will look closely at the meaning of each of the four immeasurables as well as the various contemplative practices that help us cultivate them. In this chapter we will begin by focusing on the first immeasurable: loving-kindness.

THE PRACTICE OF LOVING-KINDNESS

"Loving-kindness" (a translation of the Sanskrit word *maitri*) is the wish that all beings be happy. When I look at my great-niece Sarah, without effort I have the wish that she always be happy. Right now she is on the cusp between childhood and adolescence, and I would like her to feel pleasant, buoyant, and warm feelings of happiness all the time. I would like to see her smiling and laughing, enjoying herself and her circle of friends and family. Obviously, extending that wish to *all* beings is far more challenging, but that is what loving-kindness is ultimately about.

When we "contemplate," we make use of our thinking minds. We engage our memories and imaginations in a way that we don't when we are practicing mindfulness-awareness meditation. The name "contemplative psychotherapy" is something of a misnomer, since our emphasis is on direct experience, not contemplation. Still, it's been the name we've used for many years, and it's too late to change it now. That said, how do we contemplate the quality of mind known as loving-kindness?

Traditionally, we begin with ourselves. It can be useful to do this contemplation while sitting on your meditation seat, but it can be done anywhere. You may want to read through the rest of this section first, before trying the contemplation for yourself.

Start by remembering a time in your own life when you were happy. Think of the situation and circumstances. Where were you? Who else was there? What happened? Let go of considering how that happiness was impermanent; of course it didn't last forever. Just attend to the experience of happiness. What did it feel like in your body? What were the sensations you felt? What thoughts and images did you have? Close your eyes and simply remember as well as you can. It is fine if this one memory turns into another happy memory or even if it drifts into imagination. However you do it, try to conjure up the felt experience of happiness itself.

Then, wish that you might be happy. Use sentences like, "May I be happy. May I be at my ease. May I have what I need. May I experience peace." Repeat sentences like these, feeling free to change them, letting them be as genuine as you can. Do this for a while.

Then, begin to extend these wishes out to one other person or being. Choose someone you care about and wish that this being, too, could feel this same experience of happiness. If I choose to extend the practice to Sarah, I might say silently to myself, "May Sarah be happy. May she be safe and at her ease. May she have everything that she needs. May she have peace of mind." Feel free to use whatever names you like and make up sentences that feel personal and accurate to you. I often change the sentences as I go along. Some teachers suggest that we wish that others can experience whatever peacefulness and relief we have garnered from our meditation practice. The point is to let the practice be heartfelt, so do whatever you like to tap into the wish for this particular being to be happy.

Then, continue to expand this contemplation outward to include more beings. You might expand by starting first with other beings for whom you care deeply: family members, friends, even pets. You can do this one by one, or you can think of groups of beings. Next, you can include one or more beings toward whom you feel neutral, like the people you see at the post office or read about in the newspaper, beings who have no particular emotional charge for you one way or another. Finally, you can include those with whom you have a hard time and toward whom you typically have negative feelings. This is the hardest part of the practice, and it can be surprisingly rich. Today I think of the man who called yesterday on the phone and whose unreasonable aggression covered up some unknown pain. His aggression and rudeness led me not to hire him for a small job we needed done around our house. In my loving-kindness meditation, I wish that he were happy and relaxed. I wish that he could stop pushing people away to his own detriment.

Another way to expand the practice is geographically. You can begin with those who are nearby and expand outward to those in your region, your area of the country, the continent, and the world. You can expand into the universe itself. I find, for myself, that if I get too conceptual I lose the heartfelt quality of the practice. However, if I think of specific examples, I can expand out quite far. I think of the people on my local downtown mall who are homeless. I think of the woman who I saw standing on the road in Boudha, Nepal, with her very thin infant in her arms, begging. I remember the dogs with their ribs showing who were wandering the streets in India. I think of Iraqi children who have lost their parents and of countless parents who lost their children. It is not hard to find many beings who I wish were happy.

Wishing happiness to those who I judge very negatively is much harder. Unlike the Dalai Lama, I struggle to wish happiness to the Chinese who forced him out of Tibet. I have a hard time imagining that the Nazis who perpetrated the Holocaust should be happy. Then, I realize that if all these beings had been content and happy, the actions they took might have been different, too. With this as my motivation, I wish them the peaceful mind of ultimate wisdom. I discover that I *can* deeply wish that all beings be fully awakened, happy, and at their ease.

Generally, loving-kindness meditation is not something I would introduce to my clients, for the same reasons I choose not to teach them how to meditate (as explained in chapter 8). As a formal practice it seems more appropriate for us as therapists. However, I have had a few clients over the years who discovered it for themselves and found it helpful. Some of my clients are aware of my Naropa connection and have sought me out because of it. In some of those instances, there are times I might suggest that they consider doing loving-kindness practice.

LOVING-KINDNESS:
AN ANTIDOTE TO SELF-AGGRESSION

Chögyam Trungpa presented loving-kindness from a somewhat different angle. He talked about loving-kindness as unconditional friendliness and emphasized developing it as an antidote to the self-aggression that he saw as rampant among his Western students.[1] In contemplative psychotherapy, we define "aggression" as pushing away or rejecting experience. It is not the word we use for forceful or assertive behavior. So, self-aggression is pushing away aspects of one's own experience or rejecting oneself in some way. Loving-kindness is the opposite: it is allowing all aspects of one's experience to be recognized and rejecting none of them.

As a psychotherapist and teacher, I see self-aggression, self-hatred, and what we call "low self-esteem" as common problems. Apparently the Dalai Lama was surprised to learn that while many Western students wished to be happy, they also didn't believe that they deserved to be.[2]

B. Alan Wallace, a Buddhist teacher, scholar, and prolific author on Tibetan Buddhism, describes an incident in which American Buddhist teacher Sharon Salzberg asked the Dalai Lama about how best to introduce loving-kindness practice in America, where so many students experience "self-contempt." Apparently, the Dalai Lama was surprised because in Tibetan culture this is an unknown idea. She explained to him that while many of her students wished to be happy, they also believed that they didn't deserve to be. Often when I guide loving-kindness meditation with my contemplative psychotherapy students, I begin by asking them to think of someone they care about and only at the end ask them to wish for happiness for themselves. Once they have practiced extending loving-kindness to others, they often find it easier to include themselves. Likewise, it is not unusual for therapists to feel more comfortable and familiar with wishing good things for others and not themselves.

I find it helpful to think of Chögyam Trungpa's idea of unconditional friendliness. A really good friend is one who remains our friend no matter what. Such friends won't lie to us or reject us even if we do something they disapprove of. Perhaps they will point out our carelessness, thoughtlessness, or ill-considered behaviors, but they will remain our friends. Many of us can imagine extending that kind of friendliness to others more readily than we can offer it to ourselves.

Warmth and Nonaggression

Let's look more closely at the idea of loving-kindness as an antidote for self-aggression. Generally, when I use the term "loving-kindness," I am referring to a willingness to experience whatever arises in oneself and then letting it be what it is. So, there are two aspects to loving-kindness: having a welcoming attitude toward any experience and then not pushing it away. We could recognize these two qualities as warmth and nonaggression.

Not pushing away experience is different from liking it or judging it as positive. Loving-kindness is more like acceptance and having an open, nonjudgmental attitude. We are free to make choices based on our experiences; loving-kindness does not imply having a passive attitude. The technique of touch and go, introduced in chapter 8, is helpful in experiencing whatever arises without pushing away.

For example, I might be practicing mindfulness-awareness meditation and have a wave of intense anger arise toward my old landlord, Barry. Instead of trying to figure out why it is arising, or trying to get it to go away, or even telling myself that feeling anger is salutary, I could simply feel the direct experience in the moment. I could feel the heat arising in my chest and neck, and notice the fantasies in my mind of the scathing and clever things I would have loved to say to this man. I could just let all this be whatever it is. Without rejecting anything, I could recognize my experience just as it is and also let it be without running an internal movie starring me in the role of righteous and downtrodden tenant. Since it was nearly thirty years ago that Barry was my landlord, the whole episode is quite empty and can be let go. On the other hand, if he were still my landlord, after I finished sitting, I might choose to call or write him, or present my concerns to an attorney.

Gentleness

A point to emphasize here is the importance of gentleness, which is another possible manifestation of the friendly and nonaggressive attitude of loving-kindness. I received a lesson in gentleness for which I am still grateful. I was participating in a monthlong meditation retreat when I suddenly felt a wave of terror. Without thought, I jumped up and quickly left the meditation hall. A staff member sitting in the back, Jonathan, followed me out. "I've got to get back in there," I said. Getting back on a horse that throws you was a half-formed notion in my mind. "Gotta get back in there!"

"No," said Jonathan. "Have a cup of tea. Play with the cat. The most important thing is being gentle with yourself. Then, you can go back in the meditation hall when you're ready." I remember that lesson in loving-kindness often.

ATTITUDES MISTAKEN AS LOVING-KINDNESS

There are a number of attitudes and behaviors that are easily mistaken for loving-kindness. The first is thinking that loving-kindness is liking oneself. Liking is a form of judgment and loving-kindness is more of an experience, an attitude, not a thought or judgment. Another common error is thinking that loving-kindness is being nice to oneself. It is, of course, possible that treating oneself well could reflect an attitude of warmth and self-acceptance, but it could just as easily be a behavior that supports ego. I have had students sometimes describe to me how mindlessly watching a movie was exercising their loving-kindness toward themselves. While not condemning movies, I would have to suggest that tuning out is not the same as welcoming all experiences with a friendly attitude. It is more likely a way to reject one's direct experience.

Loving-kindness is also not a little internalized speech we give to ourselves to counter a story line about negative emotions or memories. Reminding ourselves of our successes may have a place in puncturing a mistaken view of ourselves, but it is not the same thing as the direct experience of loving-kindness.

For meditation practitioners, loving-kindness is an outcome of our practice. Sitting with ourselves and practicing moment by moment the simple discipline of being with whatever arises, letting it be, and letting it go, naturally uncovers loving-kindness. In addition, loving-kindness practice also helps us cultivate both the wish for others to be happy and also the warm and gentle quality of loving-kindness toward ourselves.

We can also cultivate loving-kindness off the cushion. While, strictly speaking, loving-kindness is not a thought, still we can make use of our contemplative, thinking minds to remind ourselves that we could have more loving-kindness toward ourselves. Sometimes just remembering that it is possible to let our experience be what it is leads, if not to an experience of loving-kindness, at least to some degree of relaxation with ourselves.

CULTIVATING LOVING-KINDNESS IN THERAPY

In contemplative psychotherapy, our aspiration is to help our clients recognize and manifest their brilliant sanity. Since "brilliant sanity" is a term for our absolute nature, it is, perhaps, completely outrageous to think of it as a treatment goal. After all, it sounds like the aim of many spiritual paths. While I certainly don't suggest giving up that aspiration and all it implies, I sometimes translate this goal into a simpler form: I am especially interested in helping my clients develop mindfulness, loving-kindness, and connection. If I feel I've lost track of what I'm trying to do, I can come back to those simple reference points: mindfulness, loving-kindness, connection.

Recognizing the Lack of Loving-Kindness in Our Clients

In contemplative psychotherapy we note that rather than experiencing loving-kindness toward themselves, many clients have a deeply held belief in their own "basic badness." I have been told that it is more common in Asia for ego-clinging to take the form of self-cherishing. In the West we are constantly bombarded with advertising that tells us how we are lacking. If only we buy the right car, the newest fashion, the most exclusive perfume, then we might be happy. We have seen how this attitude even pervades our approach to spirituality in the form of spiritual materialism. The message is that if we have the right something-or-other, we will be happy. From the point of view of loving-kindness, this is starting from the wrong end of things. Happiness is to be found in how we are, not in what we have.

In the West, ego as basic badness is quite pervasive, and we see this in our psychotherapy practice. Our clients, rather than assuming that they are workable, brilliantly sane, and have a heart of bodhichitta, are frequently convinced that they are undeserving, flawed, or damaged beyond repair. Clients who have had abusive, neglectful, or otherwise challenging childhoods often begin to believe very early that the cause of their suffering is their own badness. The adults in their lives may have taught them this directly or indirectly.

Many of us and our clients have internalized the message that we are not acceptable as we are. Members of targeted groups may have internalized the oppressive attitudes that have been directed at them. Internalized feelings of racism, homophobia, anti-Semitism, sexism, and so on are quite common. They are particularly pernicious forms of self-aggression.

One of our main therapeutic goals is to assist our clients in developing some loving-kindness, and there are a number of ways we can help them do this: through modeling, through the experience of exchange, through supporting instances of loving-kindness when it arises, and through talking about it directly.

Modeling Loving-Kindness

How we listen to our clients can model loving-kindness. Many of us have already learned to listen with a nonjudgmental and unconditional openness to whatever our clients tell us. At the same time, we show curiosity and gentleness in asking for further clarification. Simply being interested in our clients' direct experience, beyond their stories, is another way we demonstrate an attitude of loving-kindness.

Most important, our willingness to be with our clients as they experience discomfort and suffering models an attitude of loving-kindness. If we are not quick to suggest ways to escape direct experience, we show that it is possible to be with any state of mind and body. Having had the opportunity to do that, then we might choose to explore ways of working with particular states of mind or life problems.

Loving-Kindness in the "Exchange"

In chapter 7, we discussed the experience of "exchange," in which, when we are with others, we pick up directly on what they are experiencing. How we work with exchange in the psychotherapy relationship is a powerful way we indirectly support the cultivation of loving-kindness in our clients.

First, we can be practicing loving-kindness ourselves by bringing curiosity and warmth to whatever arises in our own minds in response to our clients' experiences and stories. In other words, we are willing to exchange with the clients' pain ourselves. If we do that, it will definitely affect how we respond to them verbally and nonverbally.

When Ellie, the woman I mentioned at the beginning of the book, told me about her neglectful and abusive parents, my willingness to allow sadness, anger, and pain to be present for me let me stay connected with her. It did not require that I share my experience verbally. However, if I had pushed away my experience or changed the subject even subtly, I would have conveyed to her that here too she would be neglected and alone with her pain. Needless to say, this would have had a profound effect on what could then happen in our work together—the therapist's own cultivation of loving-kindness, that is to say, is important in the unfolding of the therapeutic relationship.

A second way that the therapist's work with exchange can support the cultivation of loving-kindness has to do with the idea that exchange goes in both directions. The client picks up on our experience in the moment, too. In this case, Ellie may have picked up on the experience of loving-kindness through the exchange. That is, she may have had an experience of willingness and openness.

All therapists have probably had the experience of clients saying that something valuable happens for them in just coming and talking with their therapists. I would suggest that sometimes this occurs because of this experience of loving-kindness that clients may experience with their therapists, without their therapists ever saying anything about it. For many clients, this may be their first experience of loving-kindness, and it comes from exchanging with their therapists.

Francine came back into therapy with me after moving back into Boulder after being away for a few years. She offered that one of the reasons she had chosen to work with me was her initial feeling that I saw her as a good person. A survivor of physical and verbal abuse in childhood, she found this both appealing and a bit discomforting. I suspect that she got this impression of my sense of her through exchange. I certainly never told her that I thought she had a heart of bodhichitta, but in fact, that is how I experienced her. Still, for this to be available in the exchange, it had to be my true experience, not just thoughts I would have liked to believe. In Francine's case, her tenderheartedness and spunky curiosity were easily seen marks of her brilliant sanity.

Supporting Clients' Loving-Kindness

Finally, we can help our clients foster loving-kindness by talking with them directly about the possibility of having a more gentle or friendly attitude toward themselves. At times when clients spontaneously express loving-kindness toward themselves, I can recognize and support that by taking the opportunity to point out what they are doing and suggest how they could apply it to other aspects of their experience. Other times, I may bring up the idea myself.

For instance, I was working with Cynthia, who had been a verbally abusive mother with her own two daughters Now in her early seventies, and a recovering alcoholic, she was not only deeply regretful, she was also convinced of her essential badness. I listened for any signs of gentleness and loving-kindness that could be nurtured. As it turned out, before I had met her, Cynthia had made some amends with one of her daughters and was a very caring grandmother to her one grandson, Jeffrey. I expressed curiosity about her time with Jeffrey. She described playing games, reading stories, and just listening to him. She was tearful in describing how she herself had never received such attention from her own mother, who had been neglectful and abusive by turns. I wondered aloud whether she could be a good and gentle grandmother to herself. Cynthia liked the idea and chose a surprising practice: she began reading children's stories aloud to herself before she went to bed. After that, we had the shared reference point of "being a good grandmother" for expressing the qualities of loving-kindness to herself and others, and we returned to it again and again.

Helping our clients to develop loving-kindness in the context of the psychotherapeutic relationship can be approached in an individual way (just as our personal practice of contemplation on loving-kindness can be): both we and our clients may begin with ourselves or, if it comes more easily, we may begin with those we feel close to. In any case, having developed some experience of loving-kindness, we are then ready to naturally expand it to others. Closely related to this expansive quality of loving-kindness is the second immeasurable, compassion, which we will look at in the next chapter.

10
the second immeasurable
compassion

COMPASSION (in Sanskrit, *karuna*), the second immeasurable, is the wish that all beings be free from suffering. It is important to remember that, in this context, suffering is not simply discomfort or pain. Suffering is our struggle to avoid the direct experience of pain. Still, as we emphasized in chapter 6, on emptiness, it is critical to recognize that suffering hurts. We should not be tempted to minimize it by noting that its nature is emptiness or by seeing that it is an extra, unnecessary layer on top of pain.

Compassion has been described as "clarity tinged with warmth," and it is a close relative of the notion of loving-kindness as unconditional friendliness that we examined in chapter 9.[1] At the same time, opening ourselves to dealing with the suffering of others is more challenging than wishing that they be happy. The practice of *tonglen*, introduced in this chapter, is a "relative bodhichitta" practice that helps us develop compassion—that is, it reflects our aspiration to wake up so that we can benefit all beings.

Genuine compassion is not especially cozy. If we are truly interested in helping another to go beyond suffering, we first must be willing to be present with and acknowledge that suffering. Then we must have enough courage to go beyond what has been called "idiot compassion." Idiot compassion is the well-intentioned but ineffectual kindness that does not help others cut through their confusion but instead supports the habitual patterns and ego-clinging that perpetuates their suffering. To use a rather blatant example, it would be offering a drink to an alcoholic who is beginning to feel the pain of withdrawal. True compassion has been described as "ruthless." Another way to say the same thing is to say that true compassion doesn't care about ego. If we are to act compassionately, we may have to be willing not to be liked or even understood.

Knowing what is and is not genuinely compassionate activity in a particular situation requires us to have the clarity and openness of absolute bodhichitta and brilliant sanity. This is a tall order. Once again, we can recognize that along the path we do what we can while understanding that our aspirations may exceed our present abilities. In the meantime, we can continue our meditation and other practices to develop our inherent wisdom and compassion.

TONGLEN PRACTICE

Tonglen is the practice of "sending and taking." It is a formal practice that is done in the context of one's mindfulness-awareness sitting practice. Most simply, it is the practice of taking in suffering and sending out bodhichitta, our natural compassionate wisdom. My own sense is that when we are fully present and awake, this is what we do naturally. When we are open to the experience of exchange, we feel the suffering of those we are with. We "take" it in. If our hearts are open, we naturally feel the desire to alleviate others' suffering, and we offer or "send" out whatever we can that will help. This is, I imagine, the natural activity of the bodhisattva.

However, embodying that kind of wakefulness is not where most of us live most of the time. Tonglen provides us with a way to cultivate bodhichitta, together with its qualities of wakefulness, spaciousness, and compassion. The very things that we tend to regard as distractions from our sitting practice are extremely useful in tonglen: thought, emotion, and imagination. Tonglen can be a challenging practice because it reverses the habitual logic of ego. Instead of grasping what we'd like, we give it away. Instead of pushing away suffering, we take it in.

TONGLEN EXERCISE

There are three parts to tonglen practice. I will describe them in some detail first and then summarize them. Read through the whole description before trying it.

Step 1: Flashing on Absolute Bodhichitta

After first practicing mindfulness-awareness meditation for at least ten minutes or so, we can begin tonglen practice. We also want to allow another ten minutes or so afterward, so tonglen is sandwiched between two periods of relatively formless meditation. As we always do in sitting practice, we take a good, upright posture.

Then, we begin by "flashing" on bodhichitta. The basic idea is to abruptly open the mind to its true nature: absolute bodhichitta, or brilliant sanity. We do this for a couple of reasons. First, we are reminding ourselves why we are doing this practice at all: we aspire to develop relative and absolute bodhichitta as a living experience in our lives. We want to train ourselves so that we can be of genuine benefit to others.

Second, it is important to remember that our nature is not ego; we are not solid and separate. If we were, we could not do tonglen practice. From ego's point of view, any practice that is based on taking in suffering would be suicidal. So we need to remember from the beginning, that sending and taking is done of the foundation of bodhichitta, not ego.

How we flash on bodhichitta can be done in innumerable ways. One way is to just drop any preoccupation we have and let the mind open to a sense of vast space, beyond any concept. Alternatively, we could imagine the limitless sky or a landscape that is vast and open. One of my students recently described to me how she imagines an immense, golden meadow.

Another way is to tune in to the compassion aspect of bodhichitta. We could begin by having a sense of opening our heart to the suffering of all beings. Recognizing the limitless suffering of beings taps our immeasurable aspiration to relieve that suffering. Again, we could make use of our imagination instead, especially if recognizing limitless suffering feels too conceptual. We could begin our tonglen practice by remembering a very specific situation. I sometimes begin my tonglen practice lately by remembering Jackie, our standard poodle who died last year at the age of five after a long, mysterious illness. I flash on the body memory I have of her leaning into my shoulder the morning of her death. It never fails to open my heart.

Finally, we could also access the wisdom or clarity aspect of bodhichitta. We could let our mind open to the quality of knowingness, not limited to any particular object. As above, we could also make use of the imagination and remember an instance in which we were extremely clear, a moment when our insight and intuition penetrated deeply, and perhaps suddenly, into a situation. Recalling what that felt like can be an entry into bodhichitta, too.

So, however we do it, we suddenly shift our minds from our habitual mode into a more clear, open, or compassionate one. We don't try to hold on to that experience; we just "flash" on it briefly. Then we move into the second phase of the practice.

Step 2: Establishing the Texture

Having established the ground or foundation of the practice in step 1, we go on now and create the "feeling tone" of the practice. In this step we are not working with specific situations, but instead we are trying to get a sort of rhythm going that has a particular texture to it. Tonglen is said to "ride the breath."

Breathing in, we take in the feeling of suffering. I like to think of this as the "essence" of suffering, in the same way that a perfume might have the essence of lilac or the essence of musk. It can be helpful, in preparation for this practice, to recall a time, or times, in your own life when you were suffering. Then, remember, not so much the particular reasons you were suffering, but the bodily, emotional, and mental experience itself. Perhaps you felt heavy, hot, claustrophobic, pressured, constrained, sad, or hopeless. Don't get caught up in the words particularly; just try to conjure up the experience of suffering.

Then, when you do tonglen, you can breathe in that sense of suffering. Breathe in from all directions, through your pores, so to speak, not just through your mouth and nose. Remember that you are breathing into bodhichitta, not ego.

Someone like the Dalai Lama can breathe in this sense of suffering and feel it in his body. For beginning meditators, and those who have a more tentative sense of bodhichitta, it's all right to try to breathe suffering into a sense of limitless space. The same student who imagines the golden meadow confessed to me, on retreat, that since she began practicing tonglen, she had been breathing into herself, her limited sense body and ego. She never got past that very first breath! When I suggested that she could breathe into the golden meadow, she became quite inspired and reported later that now she could actually do the practice in a heartfelt way. The point is to do what you can actually do to let in the experience of suffering.

Having breathed in a sense of suffering, now breathe out the quality of freedom from suffering. Once again, you can prepare for the practice by thinking of times in your life when you felt relieved of suffering or when you felt open, clear, and tenderhearted. As you did with suffering, try to recall the direct experience of that time. Perhaps it felt cool, airy, open, bright, clean, or refreshing.

However you touch into these textures, continue breathing in and out, alternating breathing in the qualities of suffering and breathing out the qualities of freedom from suffering. Do this for a few minutes, up to a third of the time that you plan to do the practice of tonglen.

Step 3: Getting Specific

In this portion of the practice, we think of quite specific situations and then also expand the practice out. I usually think of this part of the practice having two subsections: step 3A and step 3B.

In step 3A, we choose some particular suffering. I have found that for many people it works best to start with whatever is most immediate for them. It could be something like a pain in one's back or a tickle in one's throat. It could an unwelcome emotion one is feeling or a sense of confusion in one's mind. Equally, it could be the suffering of someone else.

On your in-breath, breathe in that suffering. To breathe in here simply means to feel as completely as you can. If you feel confused about how to do tonglen, for example, just breathe in and feel what that feels like. You can use anything at all in tonglen: bodily sensations, emotions, thoughts, states of mind. Just breathe in whatever it is.

Then breathe out to yourself, or to whomever you have thought of, some sense of relief from that suffering. You can be as vast or as specific as you like. If you began with the experience of confusion, you could send yourself a sense of clarity, or a sense of loving-kindness about being confused, or whatever else you come up with. You could send yourself a soothing, cool drink or a hug. You could stay with this situation for a little while, letting it develop however it does. Perhaps the feeling of confusion shifts a bit into a sense of inadequacy. Breathe that in and then breathe out something like confidence or relaxation. It is best if you can actually feel what you are sending, but don't let it stop you if all you can do is imagine something. Tonglen is, after all, a practice, a way of developing ourselves. We do what we can in the moment and trust that we are cultivating our hearts.

Then, in step 3B, you expand the practice outward. You can think of others who are feeling exactly the same way you are. You might think of others who you know are confused or feeling insufficient somehow. You could breathe out to them some relief from their suffering. Again, you can be general or specific. Keep expanding out to people and beings you know and even to those you don't. As in loving-kindness practice, try to let the practice feel genuine while extending out as much as you can.

When you have expanded out as far as you can, choose another specific situation. Alternate between 3A and 3B. If at any point you become confused and find yourself, for example, breathing in relief and sending out suffering (don't laugh, we've all done it), just stop and begin again. If you can, just pick up where you left off. If you've completely lost track, just start again with flashing bodhichitta in step 1, briefly reestablish the texture of step 2, and continue on to step 3.

TONGLEN AND PSYCHOTHERAPY

As in the case of loving-kindness practice, the formal practice of tonglen is not something that would be appropriate for us, as psychotherapists, to teach our clients. We may, however, choose to include our clients in our own personal tonglen practice. Tonglen can be especially helpful in working with our own minds when we feel stuck in our work with a particular client or if we find that we are having actively negative feelings toward one of our clients. We can begin by breathing in our own distress and breathe out some spaciousness, kindness, or compassion to ourselves. We can then expand the tonglen practice outward and include the client in our meditation. Many times doing tonglen can help us let go of our own obstacles in our clinical work. Other times, it can, perhaps, give us a way of helping when we feel there's nothing else we can do. Sometimes, the next time we see such a client, we may find that our attitude has shifted a bit and that the relationship correspondingly alters as well.

Many people find that it is easier for them to practice tonglen on the spot than on the cushion. With anyone, but especially with clients, we can open to the pain they are feeling. We can even let it ride the breath as we do in formal tonglen. Then we can send, or breathe out, the relief that we long to offer to them. To the extent that we genuinely connect with either the longing to alleviate their suffering or with a quality of relief, that may be available in the exchange.

RECOGNIZING COMPASSION

As contemplative psychotherapists, we are interested in recognizing and nurturing compassion in our clients, in whatever guise their compassion takes. It may appear simply, for example, in a client who longs to alleviate the suffering of a loved one. It may appear as the distortion of compassionate action we call codependency.

Diane had long struggled with her relationship with her now-elderly mother. Her compassion appeared in the guise of being a "good daughter" and then later was hidden within intense anger. In her childhood, her mother had done nothing when Diane's father would come home drunk, yelling threats and obscenities that would terrify Diane and her younger brother. Like many children growing up with an alcoholic parent, Diane had cut herself off from her emotions. For much of her life, Diane was a dutiful daughter who attended diligently to all her mother's needs. In therapy, Diane was surprised to uncover a deep well of anger toward her mother. In addition to feeling anger about her mother's failure in the past to protect Diane and her brother, Diane also resented her mother's expectation that it was Diane's role to take care of her mother as she aged. "I'm just so mad!" she would say emphatically. "Doesn't that make me a bad daughter?" Still more resentment followed this thought.

This led to a period of distancing herself from her mother, who lives in a nearby town. Diane worked with allowing herself to touch into the anger that was never far away. She was afraid of this anger, because she had seen how destructive her father's rage had been. Moreover, she had been taught that good daughters don't get angry with their mothers.

However, as she let her experience be just what it was, she found that the more she let herself feel anger, the more tenderness she also felt toward her mother. Diane's anger was both an expression of loving-kindness for herself—after all, she had been treated quite badly and hadn't deserved it as she had been led to believe—and it was also a confused expression of clarity about her mother's failure to protect her children. Over time, Diane could see that the frail woman living nearby was a different person from the neglectful mother of her childhood. Having stopped fighting against her own experience of anger, she discovered some appreciation for her mother's pain as well as some genuine desire to relieve it. She continues to go back and forth between anger and compassion, and her relationship with her mother has a vital quality now that it lacked before. She has chosen not to express her anger to the elderly woman that her mother has become, not because she is suppressing that anger but because she doesn't see how it would benefit either her mother or herself. Together, we recognize the compassion Diane shows in most deeply wanting only to benefit her mother by making this choice.

Christina came to see me because she found herself in one relationship after another in which she was the caretaker of what appeared to be increasingly emotionally unavailable men. Some of these men had been alcoholics; others were mentally disturbed but denying their situation. Christina took care of the details of their lives, often making excuses for them to various authorities: bosses at their workplace and her own, the police, their parents. In a similar fashion, she often took on extra shifts at her work—which happened to be in the mental health field—so that her colleagues could have time off. She was exhausted and unhappy.

Our work together involved exploring not only the compassionate impulses that led her to want to help her boyfriends, her mental health clients, and her colleagues, but also the terror she felt of being alone and not needed. Christina's experience is a fine example of compassion gone astray. We could easily label her as codependent, but we might miss the compassion underlying her suffering. For the contemplative psychotherapist, recognizing and supporting Christina's fundamental compassion is as important as helping her to see how her avoidance of the pain of loneliness leads her to greater suffering. Being needed had also become part of her ego-story, which needed to be explored. Learning to tolerate the experience of loneliness became an expression of loving-kindness and compassion toward herself, since it allowed her to let go of her dysfunctional, self-aggressive identity as irreplaceable caretaker. The more she frees herself up from her helper identity, the more she may actually be able to offer genuine, compassionate help.

11

the third immeasurable

joy

THE THIRD IMMEASURABLE is joy, or as it is sometimes called more specifically, "sympathetic," or even "empathetic," joy—that is, rejoicing in the well-being of others. When I first heard that joy (in Sanskrit, *mudita*) was one of the immeasurables, I was a bit startled by the idea. Joy had always seemed like a particularly wonderful state of mind to me. How could cultivating this great experience be part of the path of cultivating bodhichitta and benefiting others? The suggestion is that rejoicing in the well-being of others opens our hearts and helps us recognize bodhichitta. As I worked with this notion, I began to recognize its truth.

When Jackie, our standard poodle who died last year, was still healthy, she would run in wide circles in the fields behind our house. She would sail into the air with all four legs stretched out, land again, and continue running only to leap again into the air. It was clear that she did it for the pure joy of it. Watching her, my heart would just lift in my chest with sheer happiness. Even now as I remember it, a smile comes to my face.

Joy is an openhearted and expansive feeling of delight. It is the opposite of being closed down, self-absorbed, and tight. As we witness the well-being of others, it is natural for us to experience happiness for them. In addition, we exchange with it and experience joy ourselves. When we turn our minds to the practices of cultivating joy, we may discover that there are many more opportunities to feel joy than we may have ever imagined.

THE PRACTICE OF REJOICING

As with the first two immeasurables, we begin to cultivate this one by attending to our naturally occurring experience. In this case, we begin by noticing the very human experience of joy in ourselves. We can do these practices either on the cushion or off the cushion. There are a couple of ways to start. One way, as Pema Chödrön describes, is to think of all our good fortune and to rejoice in it.[1] We can include anything at all in the category of things we are thankful for, from the most uplifted and sacred to the most mundane and ordinary. As I write this, I feel gratitude for the privileges in my life that have allowed me not only to hear the Buddhist teachings but also have the good health and leisure to practice them. I am so appreciative to have discovered a way of working with my mind and to have gained the knowledge that I am thoroughly workable. I think of the kindness of my father, who encouraged me to follow my curiosity. I think of my root teacher, Chögyam Trungpa, who had the persistence and patience to teach a host of confused Western students like myself. I think of my family and friends who support and challenge me.

I think of the joy of riding my bike, of playing bridge with good friends, of eating my favorite foods. I think of the delight I feel in having the opportunity to teach and to work with my clients. I am grateful to have work that feels useful. Once begun, it is easy to keep coming up with things. As I think of things, I also bring mindfulness to my direct experience. The buoyancy and tender happiness I feel is a kind of joy.

The second way to begin, suggested by B. Alan Wallace, is to think of someone you know who is joyous.[2] Perhaps you will think of a child or a bouncy kitten. Or you might think of a friend or family member and think of a time when that person was gloriously happy. Then imagine what it would be like to feel that way yourself. Identify with that being and, through empathy, feel what his or her experience might be.

When my parents reached their fortieth wedding anniversary, it was the same day that year as the Super Bowl in which, coincidentally, their local football team was playing. My sister and I gave them football jerseys with both the number forty and their last name, Kissel, on the back. When my mother opened her gift package, she got so excited that she literally bounced around with elation. She didn't know what to do first: say something, hug us, or try on the jersey. She was filled with joy. When I imagine myself feeling like that, I evoke the experience of joy.

Whichever method one uses—whether it's rejoicing in one's own good fortune or empathizing with another's experience of joy—we begin the practice of cultivating joy by simply tuning in to the direct experience of joy. Then, as we did with the loving-kindness and tonglen practices, we extend outward with the wish that others could also experience such joy. If we begin by rejoicing in our own good fortune, we can expand our practice to others by thinking of them rejoicing. This is a bit different from wishing that they are happy, as we do in loving-kindness practice. Here we imagine them feeling joy for the good fortune of others. As we continue to expand out, we also rejoice in the joy that we imagine others feeling. As before, we can extend out first to someone we love and care for. Then, we can extend out to those toward whom we feel neutral. Finally, we can try to extend out to someone toward whom we feel a lot of negativity. Obviously, this last step is the most difficult.

If we use Wallace's approach, we can try to imagine another person feeling joy about something. Then we can also identify with that person and try to see what it might be like to be in their skin. Doing this practice can help us soften what may be a one-dimensional view of that person. Again, we begin with someone we care about and extend next to someone we feel neutral toward and finally to someone we have difficulty with. Seeing that even the most difficult people can feel joy may shift our perception of them. Wallace warns us not to identify with joy that someone might feel in being harmful to another. That is not beneficial to us or even to the other person. Instead, since we are, after all, trying to arouse bodhichitta, we imagine that person feeling joy in a wholesome way. Then, we might be able to find it in ourselves to rejoice in their well-being.

Cultivating Rejoicing

Another aspect of cultivating joy is to rejoice in the accomplishments of ourselves and others. Just the other day one of my students expressed embarrassment and hesitation at the idea of acknowledging how far she had come in her clinical skills during internship. "Wouldn't that just be ego?" she wondered. Of course, that could be a possibility, but holding on to any particular way of being can be ego, including trying to be "professional" or "modest." Simply seeing how far we have come, and that we can learn new ways of being, can be an occasion for celebration and joy.

We can do the practice of cultivating joy anywhere and anytime. Whenever we see or experience something that we appreciate, we can "take in" that experience and feel joy. We can then wish that others might also have that experience.

Rejoicing as an Antidote to Jealousy

Rejoicing in the well-being or the virtues of others is also a traditional practice for working with jealousy. When I first heard of this idea, my first reaction to it was to feel reassured. "Oh, Buddhist practitioners have experiences of jealousy? It's not just a particularly embarrassing feeling that *I* have?" My next response was to think such a practice was probably beyond my abilities. Rejoice about someone else getting what I want and don't have? It seemed unlikely. Still, I would give it a try.

My opportunity to try this out came at a party. My then-boyfriend was dancing with another woman. Jealousy began to rise in my body and mind. As I sat brooding in the corner, I felt both angry and threatened. My thoughts ran along the lines of "He'll probably prefer her. She's such a good dancer and so beautiful as well. He wouldn't be dancing with her if he really cared for me. He's a creep. She's just a floozy, and I hate her. I never liked her!" Any thoughts of universal brilliant sanity were long gone, out the window. Bodhichitta? Forget it! Needless to say, I was feeling a good deal of discomfort. I probably also looked like a thundercloud had landed on top of me.

"OK," I thought. "I'll give this rejoicing practice a try." I focused my attention on the woman first. Instead of looking away, I just looked at her as she danced. I imagined what it might be like to be dancing so happily, to have such a limber body, to have long hair that I could swing around as I danced. I let myself feel how much fun that would be. Something began to shift. I turned my attention to my errant boyfriend. I imagined what it would be like to dance with this wonderful partner. I felt, as much as I could, the pleasure of dancing and feeling the beat of the music. The shifting continued. It really would be fun to be either one of those dancers. I could even wish them well—well, a little bit.

The thundercloud must have lifted some, because I was startled out of my thoughts by someone asking me to dance. I was able to just have a good time and dance myself. My previous experiences with jealousy had always been far more solid, heavy, and depressing. I'm not suggesting that this practice will always work as well as it did for me that first time, but imagining being joyful has so much more potential than the awful, thick, feeling of jealousy.

One aspect of the practice of cultivating joy that I especially appreciate is that it makes it clear that joy is a wholesome experience, one to be cultivated rather than one to be tamped down. It is, perhaps, counterintuitive that joy is a path to awakening and to letting go of ego but I invite you to try it out for yourself. When are you most able genuinely to wish for the benefit of others: when you feel joyful or when you feel miserable?

RECOGNIZING AND CULTIVATING JOY IN THE THERAPEUTIC RELATIONSHIP

As a contemplative psychotherapist, I am always interested in recognizing and supporting brilliant sanity. I am especially interested lately in how my clients express joy and in how I can support it. At the same time, I am wary of imposing some "joy agenda" on them.

Simply showing interest in what is going well, what feels good, in the lives of our clients can convey that we are interested in not only their problems, but in their whole beings. One woman I am working with sometimes compares coming to see me to taking bitter medicine. It doesn't feel good to touch into the painful emotions that she has spent a lifetime avoiding. Yet she feels this is what she wants and needs to do. There is certainly some truth in her approach. In fact, she has become better able to remain present with all kinds of painful feelings—grief, loneliness, fear, and anger—and this has freed her up to make some different choices in her life. Many times she keeps her eyes tightly closed in our sessions as she focuses on her internal experience.

She was somewhat surprised last week when I suggested that I was also interested in hearing about *any* experiences she had tapped into, not just the painful ones. She began to tell me of a time in her life when she had a delightful lover. As she described her experience, she noticed a softness and sense of delight. She and I felt connected in a way that we don't very often as we shared a sense of poignancy and tenderness.

Helping Clients Recognize Joy

When therapists help their clients to recognize the progress that they have made, they are essentially doing the practice of cultivating joy—"rejoicing in the accomplishments of ourselves and others"— as part of their clinical work. This need for finding joy can be especially important for clients who suffer with depression. In the midst of depression, it is easy to buy into a story line that things are terrible, have always been terrible, and will always remain terrible. In such a state of mind, it is quite difficult to recognize impermanence. The therapist can be helpful in holding that view even when the client is not. With some clients I can speak directly about their negative thinking patterns. With others, I might instead wait for an opportunity to mirror back the steps they have learned to take.

Patty, for example, has learned through much trial and error that if she can get herself out of the house, she will feel better than if she indulges her heavy moods and stays in bed. She has also given up a number of harmful habitual patterns, including an addiction to cigarettes. Sometimes I ask her how what she was doing a year ago differs from what she does now. Other times, she spontaneously brings it up, and we rejoice together in her progress.

Syd, another client, has a wonderful sense of humor. I have learned that if I simply wait, he will "pop" his own depression by finding something to laugh about in nearly every session. I could, of course, regard this as some kind of resistance to experiencing his pain, but from a contemplative point of view, I am interested in the sanity his humor expresses. When Syd laughs, he completely lets go for a moment. From a Buddhist point of view, we can experience only one thing at a time. Each moment is unique. When Syd experiences the joy of humor, it is impossible for him to also experience depression or pessimism. His humor may also be accompanied by a larger view: insight (or, in the Buddhist term, *vipashyana*). Sometimes he glimpses the emptiness of his habitual negative thoughts in this way. Moreover, his humor often provides us with an occasion of effortless connection.

Whenever we notice a client appreciating the joy of someone else, we can appreciate and support that. I take a good deal of interest when my clients share their joy about the accomplishments of their children, their grandchildren, and others in their lives. I often ask to see photos and delight with them in school honors, new experiences, successful rehab treatments, and anything else in which they take vicarious delight.

Seeing the Joy in Gratitude and Appreciation

Generally, recognizing and supporting experiences of gratitude and appreciation are also ways of cultivating the third immeasurable. Appreciating their love of art, music, movies, and good food can provide occasions for joining with our clients in the experience of joy. I remembered a technique I learned many years ago at an internship placement. I always thought it was pretty hokey, but it had surprising results. The technique, used in therapy groups, was to name three "new and goods." That is, the participants in group therapy were asked to identify and tell other group members three things that were recent and pleasant. Group members often struggled to come up with anything, but usually they managed to find something even if it was as small as "I made it to this meeting" or "I enjoyed breakfast this morning." In the same way that I found more and more things arising once I turned my mind to what I appreciated and felt gratitude for, these folks in therapy, often quite depressed people, also began to cheer up a bit as they identified new and goods. Once they had begun, they were likely to think of more things to report. Frequently, they discovered that as they identified the pleasant things that were happening in their lives, however minor, their moods shifted, sometimes profoundly.

More powerfully, appreciating the very people who have caused suffering in their lives can be immensely healing for clients.

Two different clients of mine found that they could appreciate, without condoning, the love that their abusive fathers showed them, once they had fully acknowledged the pain and damage that such misguided expressions of love had also caused. For one of them, it led to a profound sense of letting go. For the other, it was a relief to recognize that her father was a suffering being, not an inhuman monster.

Seemingly trivial incidents can also provide an opportunity to acknowledge and support joy. Frank told me of a small occurrence in a coffee shop. He was absorbed in his laptop computer, working on his writing, when out of the corner of his eye he saw a small child. A boy of about seven was peering over Frank's shoulder. "Hi there!" Frank said. The boy giggled. Frank found himself feeling giggly and happy, too. "He broke me out of my mind," he said. As he told me about the boy, Frank and I also shared a moment of empathetic joy.

Understanding that experiences of sympathetic joy can open up us and our clients to our inherent wisdom and compassion, bodhichitta, can encourage us to recognize and support expressions of humor, appreciation, and joy in our clinical work.

12
the fourth immeasurable
equanimity

THE FINAL IMMEASURABLE, equanimity, or *upeksha* in Sanskrit, is one that I misunderstood for years. I mistakenly thought that the idea of equanimity was to feel neutral and without feelings toward everyone and everything. I was not particularly interested in finding out how to develop it, since it seemed both impossible and unappealing. When I finally gained a better understanding of this quality, I was relieved to discover my error.

HOW TO CULTIVATE EQUANIMITY

As the final limitless quality that cultivates aspiration bodhichitta, equanimity has to do with cultivating a truly boundless attitude to all beings and all states of mind. Instead of liking, disliking, and ignoring based on our personal preferences or strategies for maintaining our own ego-stories, equanimity is about developing limitless "affectionate loving-kindness" toward all beings.[1] Moreover, equanimity means having a welcoming attitude toward all experiences and states of mind.

Open House of the Heart

The attitude of equanimity is reflected in a poem called "The Guest House," by the thirteenth-century Persian poet Rumi.[2] He describes welcoming all who arrive at the door, suggesting that we can greet even a "crowd of sorrows" graciously and invite them in. When we bring equanimity to our experience, whatever arises can be met with hospitality. Similarly, in taking the bodhisattva's vow, one invites all beings to be one's guests. I think of this approach as being a perpetual open house of the heart. Whoever and whatever shows up, we greet with "affectionate loving-kindness" and invite them in.

We understand that all of us share a common nature: absolute bodhichitta, brilliant sanity. As the Dalai Lama has often pointed out, all beings want to be happy and none wants to suffer. One way of cultivating equanimity is to recognize that if our own circumstances had been different, we might very well have responded as others have and have a life much like theirs. In his powerful poem, "Call Me by My True Names," Thich Nhat Hanh describes the death of a young woman from his native Vietnam, one of the "boat people" after the Vietnam War, who was raped by sea pirates and who later killed herself.[3] In the poem he imagines how, if he had been raised in poverty and ignorance without any opportunity to change his painful situation, he too might have become just like the pirate who raped the girl.

Misunderstanding Equanimity

It may be useful to contrast equanimity with what it is not. First, it is not, as I mistakenly thought, a way of reducing everything to some kind of indistinguishable mush, in which all experiences are the same, bland, without color or energy. I have come to call this the "mashed potatoes fallacy." Sooner or later, every year, one of my students asks a question about whether the goal of meditation is to eliminate the sharp and vivid qualities of experience. No. As far as I can tell from reading about the lives of Buddhist sages and meeting advanced practitioners and teachers, letting go of ego and its confusion leads not to a mashed-potatoes-without-salt kind of existence but to just the opposite. People become more alive and vital, like the eighteenth-century Japanese Zen poet Ryōkan, not more subdued and flat. This eccentric monk was known for spending his time sleeping, drinking sake, playing hide-and-seek with the children, and creating poetry.[4] The Tibetan Buddhist teacher and founder of the Chö tradition, Machik Lapdrön, who lived in the eleventh and twelfth centuries, was another unconventional figure. Rather than live the life expected of her as a well-born Tibetan woman, upon realizing the teachings on emptiness she demonstrated her relinquishment of all attachments by dressing in rags, keeping company with lepers and beggars, and wandering aimlessly without a fixed home.[5]

While having an attitude of equanimity doesn't mean that we see everything as all the same, bland and beige, it also doesn't mean that we find everything to be pleasant and harmonious. If we are open to all aspects of our experience, then we include it all: the sharp edges, the smooth corners, the pleasant and the unpleasant.

Another misconception about equanimity is that it is cool indifference, lack of caring about the well-being of others. Again, this is incorrect. Instead of not caring, we practice extending the affection we naturally feel for those we love to all beings. As the Buddha described it in the teaching known as the Metta Sutra, we try to develop the same attitude toward all beings that a mother might have toward her only child. The quality of warmth that is contained in bodhichitta is an important aspect of equanimity.

Having warmth and a loving attitude toward others is entirely different from feeling attached to them. This brings us into somewhat tricky semantic territory. In the psychological world, attachment is a good and necessary thing: essential to forming healthy relationships beginning in infancy. By contrast, the sort of attachment that Buddhism identifies—and regards as a problem—has to do with supporting ego by turning beings into objects and then regarding them in a fixed and limited way based on the three poisons of passion, aggression, or ignorance.[6] Equanimity, in that light, encourages us to regard all beings not as objects but rather as beings just like ourselves who have the potential to wake up to their inherent wisdom and compassion.

EQUANIMITY PRACTICES

B. Alan Wallace and Pema Chödrön both suggest that we practice recognizing how "just like me" everyone is.[7] All beings have the awakened heart of bodhichitta. Like us, not only do all other beings want to avoid suffering and attain happiness, they also, at their core, desire to benefit others.

Just Like Me

Mentally saying the phrase "just like me" in our daily lives when we see someone we feel antipathy or neutrality toward, can be a powerful practice. Instead of turning away from the homeless man begging on the highway median, I can remember that he is "just like me" and suffers from hunger and the intense heat in which he is standing. The student whose aggression I find so difficult is upset by what he sees as injustice, but he doesn't know how to skillfully bring about change. He is "just like me" in his pain. It hurts him as it would me. Needless to say, this can be a challenging practice since it is sometimes difficult to see our common ground.

We should also be careful with the "just like me" practice in another way. We might be tempted to use it as a way of ignoring—rather than being curious about and appreciating—diversity and differences. It seems to me that misusing the teachings on equanimity in that way would be a kind of spiritual bypassing. As I said in chapter 6, spiritual bypassing is the practice of avoiding emotions, conflict, or pain in the mistaken belief that it is more somehow "spiritual" to be calm or even "above it all." Regarding everyone as "just like me" as a way of downplaying the genuine pain of recipients of prejudice, injustice, and oppression is the same sort of exercise in ignorance.

A formal practice that is similar to the ones introduced for working with the first three immeasurables is to think of three people in turn: a friend, a neutral person, and an "enemy" or a person we hate or wish to reject.[8] With each of these, we contemplate how causes and conditions have come together to create the tone of our relationship with these people. If we had met them under different circumstances, wouldn't our relationships be different? If my friend had been an unfamiliar rival for a job I dearly wanted, would I appreciate her fine qualities in the same way I do now? How did I feel toward this person ten or twenty years ago? Maybe I didn't even know her. If so, I certainly didn't feel these current feelings of affection for her.

In a similar way, bringing to mind people toward whom I have no special feelings—the man who delivers my mail, the woman who holds the flag at the highway construction site—I think about how if I knew them better, I might regard them with affection or antipathy. My feelings depend on conditions and changing circumstances.

Finally, as I think of someone I don't like, someone whom I would really prefer never to see again or whom I wish would immediately leave public office, for instance, can I imagine that even these detested people desire to be happy and to avoid suffering? Can I see that they are like me? Perhaps it's possible that what I see as hideously harmful actions are, from their point of view, intended to benefit those for whom they care. If I had grown up with these people and known them my whole life, relying on them for love and protection, might I view them and their actions in a different light?

The idea of this formal practice is to show us that our deeply positive feelings for some beings and our strong negative feelings for others are the result of temporary causes and conditions. The aim is not to reduce our loving feelings but rather to show us that we could have a much larger outlook about who is worthy of affection.

The Difficult Person

Some of my students made up a contemplation that I call "the difficult person" exercise, which can be helpful in working with those with whom we are having a hard time. It's a variation on a practice that Shantideva introduces in the *Bodhicharyavatara* called "exchanging oneself for other," and it can also be used in clinical work as a kind of self-supervision practice when we are dealing with a challenging client. We begin by thinking of a person who is especially hard for us. Using our imagination, we picture the person sitting opposite us. We call up all we know about that person. Then, in our mind's eye, we identify with him or her. Now, as this person, we find ourselves looking back at ourselves. Try to get into what it is like to be this other person. Think of what matters to you. What do you care about? What do you want from this person (that is, your original self) sitting opposite you?

Imagine now, as the so-called difficult person, that you can have what you want from that person. Imagine that it is being given to you. Notice how you feel receiving it. Now, go back to being yourself, in your original seat. See what you notice. Many people discover that what the difficult person wanted was something they could easily give. Others find that they cannot. Most often, though, people discover some softening in their view of the difficult person.

Sitting Meditation

In my own experience, the most powerful practice for developing the openhearted warmth and curiosity of equanimity is the practice of mindfulness-awareness meditation that we discussed in chapter 8. This meditation practice helps us bring a welcoming attitude not only toward other people but also toward all experiences, emotions, and states of mind. As we have already seen, the practice is to include any experience, meet it with curiosity, and let it go. As we practice touch and go, we let go of our familiar habits of preferring some experiences and pushing away others. In this way we cultivate the limitless warmth and nonjudgmental attitude of equanimity.

A bodhisattva is one who has such an attitude toward all beings. As travelers on the bodhisattva path, we try gradually to develop this and the other limitless qualities. I have found that the easiest place for me to experience and practice all four of the immeasurables is in my work with therapy clients. At the same time, in the course of this work, we aspire to help our clients gradually develop their own inherent qualities of loving-kindness, compassion, joy, and equanimity.

THE CLINICAL EXAMPLE OF MACK

I recently met with a supervisee, Walt, who presented his work with a client named Mack. Mack's concerns centered around issues related to equanimity. Mack is a man in his early forties who has had a series of failed relationships. His first wife, and a number of other women with whom he has had significant relationships, have left him, complaining of his pattern of trying to control them and their lives. Mack is a successful attorney, and his confident and decisive style serves him well there, but it hasn't worked for him in his current marriage, to Dale. She has just moved out, objecting to his relentless judgments of her, her friends, and her choices. Not knowing how Dale might respond to a different approach makes Mack feel afraid and somewhat paralyzed. His biggest fear is that she would suddenly reject him altogether. Neither his habitual style nor an untried new one can assure him of the outcome he wants: Dale's love and presence.

Mack readily admits his problem with trying to judge and control others. In fact, he judges himself quite harshly for it and often resolves to change this pattern and himself.

Mack's tendency is to become attached to his judgments of himself and others as real and solid. He objectifies others, seeing only one dimension of them. He has done this with Walt as well, elevating him to the status of "perfect therapist." Mack's habitual attachment to his opinions about others is the kind of attitude for which equanimity is an antidote. In addition, his negative judgments about himself and others reflect an absence of loving-kindness.

As we talked about the possibility of showing Mack that Walt was not a "perfect therapist" but instead was a human being who is sometimes confused and uncertain, Walt noticed that he was feeling afraid that if he did so, Mack would "bolt." This paralleled exactly what Mack feared would happen if he revealed his own fears and lack of confidence to Dale. It became clear that at least one thing going on in the therapeutic relationship was Walt's exchange with Mack. Another was Walt's temptation to be seen as the perfect therapist. Once Walt recognized that second issue, though, it was easy to drop.

How can Walt help Mack to soften his judgments and attachments? How can he help him develop affectionate loving-kindness toward himself and toward others, allowing the people in his life to be human beings and not mere one-sided objects?

First, we recognized together that Walt can bring more spaciousness and loving-kindness to his own experience as he sits with Mack. Instead of feeling paralyzed by his fear that whatever he does will either support Mack's habit of judging or provide still more fuel to his fire of self-aggression, Walt can simply bring curiosity to his own and

Mack's experience and invite Mack to do the same. This can become available in the exchange as well as through modeling an attitude of loving-kindness.

Walt can ask Mack questions about himself and others that may illuminate their full humanness. He can invite him to imagine what it might be like to be another person. For example, what does he imagine it is like to be one of his law clients?

He can also be curious with Mack about any relationships in which he has experienced something other than this style of judgment and attachment. Is there, perhaps, a friend, a teacher, or a pet for whom Mack feels a less judgmental affection? If so, that can provide a useful stepping-stone or reference point.

Most important, Walt can help Mack to develop mindfulness, a "neutral observer" or "witness" function. Inviting Mack to describe things without judgment, with "just the facts," can help him become more mindful of what is happening and help him see how he embellishes what is happening with his thoughts about it. In fact, Walt has already supported Mack's interest in doing a body-scan practice in which he simply notes his bodily sensations without trying to change them. As he does this, he is also beginning to develop loving-kindness: a willingness to see what is happening and let it be what it is. Walt can suggest that Mack might bring a similar attitude to his other internal experiences, including his thoughts and emotions.

As Mack gradually develops the skills of mindfulness and nonjudgmental awareness, he may be able increasingly to tolerate the discomfort of not having a convenient label for others and of not knowing how things will turn out. Over time he may be able to soften the habit of filtering his experiences of others through the rigidly held opinions that magnify his distress about not knowing the outcome of things. He might become better able to catch his habit in action and not have to quickly judge it or himself. Instead, he might learn to simply recognize what's coming up. "Oh, you again. Hello, I know you," may begin to replace "Oh, I'm doing it again. I'll never learn. I'm stupid and hopeless."

In addition, perhaps Mack will learn that his energetic manner, which can manifest as bossiness, is not in itself a problem. The goal is not to "rein in" his basic being but rather to make friends with who he is and extend that friendliness skillfully to others as well.

WORKING WITH OUR OWN ATTACHMENTS

A couple of my students recently attended a cognitive-behavioral training workshop. Their particular trainer encouraged the participants to cultivate mindfulness and openness. My students, who by then had been practicing mindfulness-awareness meditation for at least three years, were distressed by the casual assumption that those things could be simply heard about and then applied without some kind of dedicated mindfulness practice. They were outspoken in their description to me of how they and other therapists may become attached to particular clients or to specific agendas to the detriment of their clients.

Their reactions highlight two issues in working through our own attachments. First, they were attached to their own understanding of mindfulness meditation. As a result, they were judgmental in their view of the workshop leader. At the same time, they also accurately recognized how easy it is to underestimate the difficulty of cultivating the mindfulness and awareness that lead to genuine equanimity and letting go of our attachments.

A regular mindfulness-awareness meditation practice provides an ongoing opportunity to recognize our attachments. The longer I continue my practice, the more I see how very quickly I attach my preferences to all sorts of things, not least to my clients and their decisions. Alice is planning a vacation. I am worried that she hasn't thoroughly thought through the implications of traveling with her unreliable boyfriend. Like a mother hen, in my mind I am conjuring up all sorts of ways that she will be unprotected. He may lead her into unsavory situations in his quest for recreational drugs; he might take off for days at a time and leave her alone in a foreign country. He does these things here; he could certainly do them elsewhere. I am attached to my own judgment as superior to Alice's. Moreover, I am attached to my view of Alice as a helpless victim.

In my sitting meditation, as these worries arise, I touch my fear, let myself experience it, and then, recognizing the story I have made up, I let it go. As I continue to practice, I recognize that my thoughts and fears are just that: my thoughts and fears. Perhaps I can bring a more open mind to my next session with Alice. Maybe I can actually see whether my pet theories have any ground in reality. Then, and only then, might I have something useful to offer to Alice in support of her own brilliant sanity.

Part Three
engaging in bodhisattva activity

Just like space
And the great elements such as earth,
May I always support the life
Of all the boundless creatures.

—*Shantideva,* A Guide to Bodhisattva's Way of Life

13

generosity
the first of the awakened actions

HAVING BEGUN to cultivate aspiration bodhichitta through the practices of the four immeasurables, the prospective bodhisattva starts to engage in action in the world. For contemplative psychotherapists, as for other aspiring bodhisattvas, this means learning about and starting to apply the teachings on the six "awakened actions" (or in Sanskrit, *paramitas*).

THE SIX AWAKENED ACTIONS

The "awakened actions" (also called "transcendent actions") of a bodhisattva are actions that transcend ego and its confusion. The more we are able to let go of our mistaken notions about ego, and thus uncover our inherent bodhichitta, the more our actions spontaneously manifest as the six awakened actions: generosity, discipline, patience, exertion, meditation, and wisdom. For bodhisattvas who fully manifest bodhichitta, these actions are simply their natural behavior and activity in the world.

The first five awakened actions are usually described as "skillful means" (in Sanskrit, *upaya*). That is, they are compassionate actions that benefit beings. The sixth awakened action is wisdom (or in Sanskrit, *prajna*). More specifically, the wisdom of the sixth awakened action is the "discriminating awareness" that sees and understands emptiness. In the Buddhist view, skillful means and wisdom work together and are regarded as inseparable. Without the wisdom that clearly sees all aspects of a situation, our actions are likely to be unskillful or even detrimental. On the other hand, if we have wisdom without compassionate skillful means, we will have no way to actualize our aspirations to be of help.

As we have already discussed, it is important when studying the teachings on emptiness to keep in mind the First Noble Truth: the truth of suffering. If we don't do that, we might mistakenly dismiss suffering as somehow not real. I suspect that this may be why the first five transcendent actions, with their emphasis on compassionate action, are presented first. It may be better to try unskillfully to be of benefit than to have insight without compassion.

The activities described by the six awakened actions are fruitional; they describe how a fully awakened bodhisattva participates in the world. Although they are presented separately, they are really just different aspects of skillful and compassionate engagement in the world. The awakened actions are also practices that we can undertake in order to develop what we have called "active" or "applying" bodhichitta. Whenever we glimpse their occurrence, we are seeing evidence of bodhichitta and brilliant sanity. They are practices that we can undertake now ourselves, and they are also behaviors that we can recognize and support in our clients. As the manifestation of bodhichitta and brilliant sanity, awakened actions are actually natural to us. At the same time, the more we are in touch with our inherent nature, the more our day-to-day functioning becomes that of awakened action.

"REFRIGERATOR PRACTICE"

When I teach the practice of awakened actions in class, I use a gimmick that I have adapted from an idea of a colleague, Victoria Howard. I hand out a packet of "paramita pages." On each page is the name of one of the awakened actions, together with a brief description of it. The students are asked to post these pages somewhere in their homes where they will see them frequently. Many put them on their refrigerator doors, and I think of this practice, myself, as "refrigerator practice." Others tape them to their bathroom mirrors or next to their home computers. The idea is that for the week during which we are studying a particular awakened action, the students are reminded to pay special attention to their own experience of the presence or absence of that awakened action in their daily life. Then, in class and in short papers, the students report on their week's experience .

One of my students came up with a variation on this practice. She wrote the name of each awakened action on many small pieces of paper and then secreted them all over the place. Whenever she came across one, it would remind her to attend to that awakened action. She tucked these "awakened action reminders" into her wallet, into her dresser drawers, in shoes in her closet, in her school notebooks, in her glasses case, and in her kitchen cabinets.

You might like to try this practice. Just write the name of one of the awakened actions on a sheet of paper and post it where you will see it. Then, throughout a period of time you've designated, just notice when you are, for example, acting generously and when you are, instead, behaving stingily. Just bring curiosity and loving-kindness to your experience. Try not to judge what you notice; just treat it as research. Simply bringing mindfulness to each awakened action in this way will naturally affect your daily experience. See what happens.

AWAKENED GENEROSITY

Dana, or generosity, is the first awakened action. As we continue our sitting practice and our work with the four immeasurables, we increasingly strengthen our deep desire to be helpful to other beings. One of the first ways this manifests is as the wish to act generously. The action of awakened generosity is giving and offering to others.

For instance, in May 2008 a huge cyclone swept through Myanmar (Burma). Although the exact death toll may never be known, estimates have suggested that as many as a million people were killed and several million were made homeless and without resources. Like many other people, as the tragedy was unfolding I went online and made a donation to one of the organizations providing emergency relief. Probably none of us knows any of the victims personally or expects to be recognized by them for our donations. Still, such extensive suffering readily evokes our generosity. Recognizing the suffering of others leads naturally to wanting to give some assistance.

While we respond to the needs of others, we can also recognize emptiness. There is a Buddhist teaching known as "threefold purity" that applies to all of the awakened actions, including generosity. It reminds us that all phenomena are interdependently arising by teaching that in all actions there is neither a separate actor nor a separate action nor a separate recipient of the action. Instead, they are all dependent upon one another and cannot be said to exist independently. I might easily have regarded my donation to the Burmese relief agency as something that I, a separate, solid person, was giving to some other solid, separate beings. Remembering threefold purity helps us to release any tendency we may have to create ego or develop pride based on our generosity. As with all of the bodhichitta teachings, the idea is not that we are higher than those to whom we make offerings but that we are all the same in our desire to be happy to avoid suffering.

I remember being taught as a child that the highest form of charity is anonymous giving. In a similar way, awakened generosity is about being generous in a fashion that does not seek any credit, reward, or acknowledgment at all for the giver. Like many others, I'm sure, I recognize again and again some niggling desire to be recognized for my generosity. Seeing this, I know I have a good deal further to go on the Mahayana path.

The Mahayana teachings describe three kinds of awakened generosity. Although different teachers and sources give them varying names, for our purposes here I will refer to them as (1) material generosity, (2) the gift of courage, and (3) the generosity of teaching.

Material Generosity

Providing beings with the things that they need is the first kind of generosity. This "material generosity" can include donating money, food, time, skills, or anything else that leads to beings getting what they require. As therapists we may offer material generosity by seeing a client for a reduced fee, offering an additional session, or being available by phone or on a pager.

The Gift of Courage

The second kind of generosity, the gift of courage or fearlessness, is one that I think is particularly relevant to psychotherapy and counseling. Supporting our clients' brilliant sanity can lead them to discovering their own unconditional confidence and courage. Courage is not the same as the absence of fear, but it begins with the ability to directly experience fear and not lose our mindfulness and loving-kindness.[1] As contemplative psychotherapists, we could take the perspective that we are offering the gift of fearlessness whenever we model openness or encourage our clients to be present with any challenging feelings, both unpleasant and pleasant. For our clients to learn that they are workable and worthy, just as they are, is a potentially life-changing gift.

I have been working recently with Rachel, for example, who is exploring childhood sexual abuse. She is saying some things out loud for the first time in her life. Revisiting the few memories she has of her father coming into her room and demanding displays of affection from her is both frightening and revolting to her. We spend a good deal of time bringing mindfulness to what Rachel experiences in her body in the present moment as she recalls these memories. Like many abuse survivors, she has a facility for dissociation. She readily numbs out and doesn't feel much at all. We have found that she can more easily stay in touch with her sensations if she also stays in contact with me. She maintains eye contact and reminds herself that this is 2008 and that she is in my office. At the same time, we work with mindfully backing off from feelings that are too intense right now. In that way, Rachel is learning to practice courageous mindfulness as well as loving-kindness.

The Generosity of Teaching

The third kind of generosity, the generosity of teaching the dharma, may seem unrelated to psychotherapy at first glance. While the bodhisattva teachings on this kind of generosity refer to the teachings of the Buddha (that is, the dharma), as therapists we serve as teachers (whether overtly or indirectly), for instance in the way we are constantly responding to one thing rather than another. As we do that, we are teaching our clients what we deem worthy of attention. Even if we sit in silence and let our clients choose what to talk about, we are teaching a value in doing that. If we subscribe to an understanding of human nature as being inherently characterized by bodhichitta and brilliant sanity, as described by the Buddhist teachings, we may be teaching the dharma to our clients whether we do so consciously or not. I would suggest that it is essential for us personally to clarify our own views so that we know what we are teaching our clients. Then it is up to us to decide in any particular clinical situation whether we will be direct about that or not.

Every time I ask a client to pay attention to the experience of an emotion, as I do with Rachel, I am teaching something about mindfulness. When I demonstrate nonjudgmental curiosity, I am modeling equanimity. When I hear that my client doesn't know how to proceed with a particular dilemma, and I don't offer a list of suggestions, I am supporting not only his or her brilliant sanity but also modeling that openness and not knowing are acceptable options. Not insisting that a client choose a way of being and stick to it is a lesson in egolessness.

PERSONAL PRACTICES IN AWAKENED GENEROSITY

Here are two practices that we can do ourselves to develop our own awakened generosity.

Giving Away Rehearsal

A simple practice that we often do in class is to experiment with the sense of giving some cherished object away. Start by holding something you value in your hand. Notice how it feels there and notice your attachment to the object. I often use a gold watch I bought on a trip to Europe when we do this exercise. I have all sorts of memories and feelings associated with this watch, and I notice what arises as I hold it in the palm of my hand. Then, mindfully, release your chosen object into your other hand and notice the action of letting go with one hand and of receiving with the other. You can shift it back and forth from one hand to another. It is a small beginning in working with the obstacles to generosity: attachment and miserliness.

In class, we pass our precious object to another person, again noticing both our experience as we let go of our own item and also as we receive someone else's. Then, we repeat the action a number of times and pass our belongings around the circle to people even farther away. As my watch gets farther and farther from me, I continue to track my experience. Silly as it sounds, I notice the anxiety that begins to whisper in me, "What if it gets broken? What if I don't get it back?" As cell phones and jewelry come into my own hands, I realize that others have similar attachments. Eventually, we pass our items back toward ourselves, and I notice the relief and even "grabbiness" that arises as my watch comes closer and finally returns to me.

Offering Practices

One beautiful and traditional Buddhist practice for cultivating an attitude of generosity is to make a mandala offering. *Mandala* is a Sanskrit word that, in this context, means a symbolic representation of the whole world. In this practice we emphasize all the good qualities of our own worlds that we enjoy and usually would even like to possess. Using our imaginations, we conjure up an abundant display of good things that please all the senses. We think of beautiful visual objects: clothing, fine art, flowering trees, vast expanses of natural splendor. We imagine pleasant sounds: a Mozart clarinet concerto, the songs of meadowlarks, the laughter of a baby. We add the wonderful aromas of lilacs in the spring, the subtle perfume of an old lover, the smell of burning juniper, the aromas coming from the kitchen during our favorite holiday. Then we think of delicious foods: the smooth wonder of chocolate, the fiery sting of spicy chili, the warm satisfying flavors of our personal comfort foods. Finally, we call up the sensations of lovely textures: the softness of old blue jeans, the rough wetness of a dog's tongue affectionately licking our hand, the suppleness of silk. We imagine everything we can think of, and we practice giving it all away to anyone and everyone who might enjoy it. If you try this practice, use your imagination to think of all kinds of things that you, yourself, delight in and imagine not only giving them away but also others receiving them.

Another way to do an offering practice is mentally to practice giving away anything pleasant that comes to us. When I am about to dig into a great breakfast out at a restaurant, I can think, may all beings who are hungry have such a wonderful meal. May all beings feel this happy at being in the company of such good friends. When I arrive home at the end of a busy day, I can think, may all beings have a safe and welcoming home.

CULTIVATING GENEROSITY
IN OUR WORK WITH CLIENTS

In our work with clients, not only do we have the opportunity to practice generosity toward them, but we also may help them cultivate their own generosity as well. My client Ruth offers a good example of this possibility. In many ways, Ruth was one of the most challenging clients I have ever worked with. One of the ways that Ruth was difficult for me was her frequent criticism. She was often unhappy both with what I said and what I didn't say. "Tell me what to do! Don't you have any ideas? Didn't you spend years in training? You should be able to help me!" If I became hooked into offering advice, she would be dismissive in her rejection of it. "Is that the best you can come up with? I think I'd better find another counselor." She never quite crossed the line into becoming abusive. Despite saying frequently that she would leave, she kept coming. She was always on time and prompt in paying me. If I inquired about what she got out of coming, she would just say that I was helping her. I was often at a loss about how to proceed.

Over the months we worked together, it became apparent that much of her sanity resided in her generosity. She had a passionate interest in photography, and one day she brought me a gift of three framed photographs she had taken. Each one was a careful composition of a beautiful Colorado scene: a winter streambed, an autumn forest, a hawk on a railing peering out at the viewer. She had matted them herself in colors that complemented the photographs. She was justifiably proud of her work and pleased to offer it to me.

I considered not accepting the photographs, since I could easily have interpreted them as some new manipulation. Many schools of psychotherapy discourage accepting any gifts from clients, suggesting that to do so adds unnecessary confusion to the relationship. On the other hand, the teachings on the bodhisattva vow specifically say that refusing a gift deprives the giver of the opportunity to practice generosity. Once again, with Ruth, I found myself not knowing what to do. After a brief moment of hesitation, I accepted her offering, believing that it was better to err on the side of her brilliant sanity. I shared my appreciation for the quality of her work, and she was delighted at my response.

She sometimes brought in other small gifts: a miniature stocking filled with candy at Christmastime, a little stuffed toy bear, a card for New Year's Day. She continued to seesaw between telling me how useless I was and praising me as the only one who truly cared about her. Without getting into the many different ways we could theorize about Ruth, let me just say that one of the main ways I worked with Ruth was by supporting her generous instincts.

There are two confused ways that generosity frequently manifests, and Ruth showed both of them. On the one hand, she was often proud and arrogant, placing herself above me and others in her life. On the other hand, she frequently doubted that she had anything worthwhile to offer anyone. Recognizing these as the flip side of the wisdom of generosity, I did my best to reflect her underlying sanity.

For example, when she expressed concern about whether she should volunteer, through her church, to work with teenagers interested in photography, I asked her not only about her self-doubt but also what inspired her to consider teaching photography to these teenagers. As we investigated the latter, she tapped into the confidence she had in her photographic skills and into her desire to share what she knew with others.

Sometimes it was a practice of generosity for me to keep showing up to meet with Ruth. The possible exchange with her self-doubt is more apparent to me now as I write this than it was at the time.

Perhaps we could say that it was generous of both of us to keep hanging in there with each other despite our mutual difficulties.

Paying attention both to how I was or was not generous with Ruth, as well as how she showed generosity, brought the practice of transcendent generosity into our relationship and into our work together.

Often our clients are extremely generous with us, teaching us how to be better therapists. One of my colleagues, Robert, works with James, a veteran of the Iraqi war, who suffers from intense post-traumatic stress disorder. When James first came into therapy with Robert he explained that he wanted help for himself in coping with the difficulties he experienced with flashbacks, insomnia, and other symptoms of PTSD. More important, though, he went on to say that his main goal in therapy was to train Robert in how to be a good helper, not only for James himself, but also for all of the other soldiers who suffered with combat-related PTSD. In their work together, James often stops and carefully describes exactly what he experiences and what he has discovered that helps him to work with it. He allows himself to tap into extremely painful and frightening places within his present experiences and past memories with the expressed wish to give the full benefit of these experiences for Robert's training. He could be said to be manifesting the generosity of courage as well as the generosity of teaching, both to Robert's future clients as well as to Robert himself. Robert feels honored by James's generosity and deeply appreciative of his fearlessness.

14
discipline
the second of the awakened actions

IT WAS 8:00 in the evening, and my home phone rang. When I answered, Marge was on the line. "I've gotta talk to you! My daughter Valerie has just left her kids here, and I think she's going to take off with that drug dealer again!" In the background I could hear children wailing. Marge sounded panicky. I had no doubt that she was deeply afraid and at her wits' end; my heart went out to her. What, though, was I going to do?

Marge was a client of mine from the local mental health center. I had been assigned her on a short-term basis to work on "boundaries." She had shown up at our first appointment with her two young grandchildren in tow. I told her that we couldn't meet with the children there and that next time she would have to come by herself. She came again with the children to our second session. I repeated that we couldn't meet with the kids, and we scheduled another appointment. Since then, we had met a few times on our own. Now, she was calling me at home, a violation of the mental health center's rules. As a long-time client of the center, she was well aware of the rule.

"Marge," I said. "You can't call me at home. You'll have to call the crisis line."

"But, I need to talk to you right *now*!" she said. She had shifted from fear to anger. "I need you! Valerie is—"

"No," I interrupted. "You'll have to call the crisis line." The words of the bodhisattva vow began to run uneasily in my mind. *May I be a protector for those without one.* I gave her the crisis number, said that

I would see her later in the week at our regular appointment, and hung up.

May I be a bridge, a boat, and a ship . . . May I be all things that anyone may need, but don't call me at home? I felt extremely uncomfortable.

I went to meet Marge at our scheduled appointment, wondering if she would show up. If she came, I expected that she would be furious at me. To my surprise, she was not only there on time and without the kids, she was beaming. "I told Valerie that she can't just drop the kids off at my place without asking me first if it's OK!" She was thrilled about setting this boundary with this daughter who had long taken advantage of her. As it turned out, my setting a boundary with Marge had somehow given her permission to go ahead and say no to Valerie.

THE MEANING OF AWAKENED DISCIPLINE

I often think of this incident with Marge when I contemplate the teachings on the awakened action of discipline (Sanskrit: *shila*). This awakened action teaches us to act in ways that benefit others and to refrain from behavior that harms them. It is easy to mistake the teachings of the first awakened action, generosity, as telling us to do whatever someone asks of us. The second awakened action teaches us to refrain from what has been called "idiot compassion," or as I sometimes think of it, "idiot generosity." True discipline requires that we say no as well as yes. In therapy, learning to say yes and no means working with setting limits, boundaries—for the therapist and also for the client.

If I had stayed on the phone with Marge, I would have been saying, in effect, "I will break the rules for you. I will take your side against the whole mental health center." Or, in psychological language, "I will split with you against them." Furthermore, I would have sent the message that I was unreliable. I had already presented myself as a staff member of the mental health center, one who followed its rules. Now I would be saying, "No, you can't know if I'll do what I've said I will do." As it turned out, of course, my modeling of good boundaries was apparently beneficial to her in a way I had not even thought of.

When I introduce the topic of "discipline" in class, there is often a restless stirring in the room. I usually ask people what their experiences and associations are with this word. "Punishment," "following rules," "no sex," "giving up what I want," and "rigidity" are common responses. No wonder uneasiness arises.

Discipline on the bodhisattva path is not about being "good." It is about doing what is appropriate to the moment. The word *appropriate* is another tricky one. Appropriate to what? Sometimes this word conjures up a sense of being proper and following an external set of rules. Here, though, "appropriate" asks, "Based on being present in this very moment and everything you know about this situation, what would be beneficial right now?" Obviously, this is not easy to discern. In chapter 21 we will discuss the sixth awakened action, the wisdom that enables us to discriminate between what is genuinely useful in this moment and what is not. Since most of us have not fully developed this type of wisdom, however, the discriminating awareness we bring to the practice of awakened discipline may mean being willing to not know, to not just follow a recipe. By letting our minds be somewhat open in this way, we may be able to tap into a deeper wisdom of at least seeing what is needed. Often we will never know if we have made a good choice. With Marge, I was fortunate to have some indication that my actions had been useful, but more often, we really do not get clear feedback.

As therapists, we may be told by the client that what we have done has been helpful, but there can be myriad reasons why a client may say that. One common reason we receive a good "review" is that we have supported a client's habitual pattern and not made them feel uncomfortable. No wonder the bodhisattva aspires to attain full awakening in order to know how to benefit beings. Still, we do what we can with what we have right now.

CULTIVATING DISCIPLINE IN THERAPY

For therapists and their clients, there are several clinical applications of awakened discipline, including setting sane boundaries, the practice of confession, and working with codes of ethics.

Setting Boundaries

A common issue in counseling and psychotherapy is the setting of boundaries. It is an issue both for the therapist and also for the client. At the beginning of therapy we establish some boundaries having to do with confidentiality, payment, starting and stopping times, and so on. Clients bring questions to therapy about boundaries in their lives: working with their job situations, their families, and their friends. Like Marge, they may need to learn how to say no.

A dilemma may seem to arise when we put together the idea of setting boundaries and the Buddhist view of egolessness. How can we be setting up boundaries for a nonexistent self? Haven't we just learned that there is nothing to protect? As we have seen, from a relative point of view we still have a sense of ourselves as existent even though our nature is empty from an absolute point of view. As I see it, our challenge is to set boundaries in such a way as to support waking up, not to enhance further our sense of solidity.

While we may crave the security of solid, unchanging boundaries, often we need to be open to changing them in accordance with what is actually most beneficial. All therapeutic approaches (as well as the legal system) recognize that there are times when even the boundary of confidentiality must be breached to protect the well-being of our clients. The bodhisattva approach is still more unconstrained. At its most outrageous, the bodhisattva's practice is to do whatever is needed without regard to his or her own safety, including feeding a hungry tiger with his or her own body. Most of us are not ready for such selfless heroism; still, the idea is to shift our allegiance toward wakefulness rather than toward the false security of ego.

A favorite therapy boundary for my students to disagree about is the question of starting and ending on time. On one side there is the commonsense wisdom of letting clients know what they can count on. If we end on time, clients are free to bring up scary or painful topics near the end of sessions in the certainty that they will not have to go into them too deeply for now. Sometimes, as therapists we even make this behavior overt by noting it aloud.

On the other side is the view that an aspiring bodhisattva bases his or her actions on what is needed in the moment. An emergency is an obvious occasion when we may choose to ignore the usual boundaries. But are there other times with particular clients? I had one student who insisted that his own therapist's allowing a session to run significantly over time had given him the message that he mattered. It had created a crack in the very solid armor of his depressive self-narrative and allowed in some glimmer of loving-kindness. This, he argued, was the point, after all. Wasn't it?

The Practice of Confession

An important practice that can be associated with the awakened action of discipline is the act of confession. Once again, for some students and readers, this may be yet another loaded concept. We can understand confession, in the Buddhist context, as practicing discipline of speech. The idea is that we name aloud those emotions, thoughts, and behaviors that seduce us back toward ego-activity, toward our comfort zone, and away from what we actually know is helpful. This helps us recognize and bring awareness to what we do. It is not about creating guilt or feeding self-aggression. Instead, it is a practice in courage.

In the early days of the Buddha, monks would confess transgressions of their vows in front of their community of fellow meditation practitioners on a regular basis. In the absence of community or friends who share one's practice, a Buddhist practitioner might confess one's failures to uphold the bodhisattva vow to benefit others aloud in front of an image of the Buddha or a teacher.

The person to whom a modern layperson would "confess" his or her misdeeds is likely to be a friend, a partner or, not surprisingly, a therapist. Many times clients come to see us for just this reason: they need to tell someone what they have been doing, feeling, thinking. Part of the power of both confession and therapy is exactly this speaking out loud to another person. If you have any doubts on this score, try saying out loud something you feel a bit uncomfortable about— right here as you read by yourself. Then, see what happens as you imagine saying it to someone else. Finally, you could actually say it to someone. For most people, the intensity tends to increase. Therapists make use of this phenomenon sometimes when they titrate the intensity of an interaction with a client. We might increase the intensity and liveliness of the interaction by asking the client to say something directly to us, or we might lower it by asking the person, instead, just to imagine saying it.

Recently I led a conference program for a group of pastoral counselors. On the way to the program, the man who picked me up at the airport, a Christian minister, engaged me in a conversation about confession. His take on it was similar to what I have found in my own experience based on my Buddhist practice. Confessing, he said, helps people to recognize and acknowledge their responsibility, to do what they can to make amends, and then to let go and move on with their lives. It was related, he said, to forgiveness.

Shantideva presents a teaching regarding confession, known as the "four powers of confession," that in my experience has particular application to psychotherapy. Different commentators present the four powers in differing orders, but they are, briefly: the power of regret; the power of reliance; the power of remedial action, or antidotes; and the power of promise. To illustrate, I'll tell you about Jerry, a man in his late forties, who had long carried a burden of pain about the killing of small animals he had done as part of a laboratory job he once held.

The Power of Regret. The first power, regret, begins with seeing how one's actions have caused suffering or harm to others. Jerry readily saw this. Sometimes it is the work of therapy to help clients see how their actions affect others, but that was not an issue here. Jerry felt not only regret but also guilt for killing rats, mice, and rabbits in his former job.

Allowing oneself to feel the pain of regret is a step toward healing and loving-kindness. Jerry could let himself directly feel the pain of deep regret. Unfortunately he could also easily turn regret and sadness into self-aggression. As we have already seen in the chapter on loving-kindness, self-aggression is a pernicious and difficult problem, and it often arises when clients recognize their harmful habitual patterns. Jerry was well-practiced in believing his internal narrative about how hopelessly bad he was. One manifestation of his self-aggression was his seeming inability to take care of his health: he was overweight and suffered from a variety of ailments. In therapy and between sessions, Jerry practiced feeling regret and not cutting his direct experience of pain by turning it into a self-aggressive story.

The Power of Reliance. The power of reliance has a traditional meaning. In the Buddhist tradition, one relies on what are known as the "Three Jewels": the Buddha as an example of wakefulness, the dharma as the Buddha's teachings, and the sangha (the community of practitioners). Clearly, I don't talk about the power of reliance with my clients in these particular terms. Instead, I express interest in what they already rely on: what people, what beliefs, what communities do they turn to for support and to reflect their goodness back to them? Often, I am one of the people they rely on. One aspect of this power is the realization that none of us has to try to take care of everything on our own.

Paradoxically, therapists and other helping professionals are notorious for not seeking out help for themselves. The power of reliance suggests that we, too, need to seek support from our supervisors or peer consultants, our friends, our family, and our spiritual traditions.

My client Jerry identified some practices from his childhood religion that helped him remember that he was not basically bad: it was helpful for him to remind himself that he was a child of God and that he might, just might, be eligible for forgiveness.

The Power of Remedial Action. The third power, the power of remedial action, or antidotes, refers to all the actions and practices we can undertake to "purify" or rectify our actions. Again, in the Buddhist tradition this tends to run to performing Buddhist rituals or repeating mantras. In psychotherapy, it refers to any and all interventions we make or actions the client undertakes to make amends when possible or to let go of harmful beliefs, attitudes, and behavior. For Jerry and me, this meant designing a specific ritual that we then performed together in my office. Jerry was a Naropa graduate, and he had taken a class in creating rituals. I, too, have an interest in ritual, so together we discussed in great detail how we could design a ritual to address Jerry's feelings of regret, guilt, and self-aggression. He set the room up in a particular way, wrote some personally meaningful liturgy, and identified some religious songs. He brought in a large toy stuffed rabbit and, at one point, tears streaming down his face, asked forgiveness of it as a representative of all the animals whose lives he had taken.

The Power of Promise. The last power is the power of promise. Simply, one promises not to perpetuate whatever the problem habit has been. For Jerry, he had already long ago given up the laboratory job, but he chose to also try to benefit other animals by caring for his pet cats and also contributing to animal protection charities.

In the few sessions we had after doing the ritual, Jerry reported a sense of relief, renewed energy, even joy. He had glimpsed the magic of his awakened heart.

The four powers can be helpful in working with any habits, including addictions, and often the four stages of the practice need to be repeated many times.

Discipline and Professional Codes of Ethics

A third application of the transcendent action of discipline to therapy is the whole domain of ethics. When I read the American Psychological Association (APA) or the American Counseling Association (ACA) codes of ethics, I am struck by their emphasis on protecting the client's welfare. Instead of understanding these sometimes complicated documents as a set of arbitrary rules, I find it can be inspiring to see how the bodhichitta of psychological counseling disciplines is expressed in these guidelines on how to be compassionate and not harmful.

For example, in the APA and other professional codes, there is an item that says that psychologists will see some clients for reduced fees. Another ethical guideline says that we will never "abandon" a client. In other words, even if we cannot work with a client ourselves (it is unethical, for example, to work with a client whose issues require expertise that we do not have), we still do our best to refer the person to someone else who can help.

Sometimes I feel I walk a very narrow edge in trying to meet both the ethical requirements of my profession and the demands of the bodhisattva teachings. Lisa arrived at our very first appointment smelling of alcohol although she was a member of a religion that did not allow it. She denied that she'd been drinking, but it was fairly obvious. Over time it became clear that she had a lot of pride, and it often got in the way of her admitting her problems directly. For example, although she hinted that a high school custodian had sexually assaulted her, she insisted that it was her own fault for losing a bet about how many foul shots she could make in a row. She utterly refused to discuss it further.

More troublesome was her frequent habit of calling the office in an inebriated state and leaving angry, sometimes incoherent, messages threatening to harm herself or terminate therapy. After any number of conventional interventions, including sending the police to her home to check on her welfare, I had an idea that sat on the edge between being clearly ethical and questionably so, but had a chance, I thought, of meeting Lisa's needs.

At our next session, I told Lisa that I could see that her drinking was harming her, and that I felt that by continuing to see her in therapy, I was supporting this harmful behavior. I explained that I had gotten to know her well and cared for her, but that I could no longer, in good conscience, be her therapist. I would not abandon her, though, and I would continue to see her twice weekly as we had been doing. I would not, however, let her pay me. I had also written all of this out in a letter and offered it to her.

She was furious—among other things, she had never admitted to the drinking. Grabbing the letter, she stormed out of the office. The next day I got a phone call. Lisa said she could not see me without paying me, and she didn't want to stop coming. She made me an offer: she would stop drinking for six months and then we would see. I accepted the offer. In fact, in the next six months, Lisa kept her promise, and did some remarkable work. She remained sober after the six-month period as well. While this intervention did not, strictly speaking, violate any ethical boundaries since I was not abandoning Lisa, it could have appeared to her that I was in fact abandoning her by refusing to be her therapist. My approach was certainly not a conventional one. Note that this strategy arose from my relationship with Lisa, and I am certainly not recommending it as a model for any other client.

These three topics—setting boundaries, practicing confession, and working with codes of ethics—are just some of the many ways that the teachings of the awakened action of discipline may be applied to the practice of psychotherapy. In some sense everything we do is included in the awakened action of discipline. As therapists we are always endeavoring to help our clients to refrain from what causes their suffering and to cultivate what enhances their sense of health and well-being.

15

patience
the third of the awakened actions

As WE SAW in part 2, cultivating the four immeasurables has to do mainly with working with our own attitudes. The awakened actions, too, emphasize working with our minds, but at the same time they also involve us in interacting with others. The third awakened action (in Sanskrit, *kshanti*), which is usually translated as "patience" or "forbearance," teaches us how to work with our own and others' aggression.

From a Buddhist point of view, the way to benefit others is to support their discovery of how to stop perpetuating their own and others' suffering as well as how to cultivate their own happiness. Remembering that the Buddhist understanding of the cause of suffering is that it is the product of our tenacious clinging to a false sense of self and reality, as psychotherapists we may often be in the position of gently, or not so gently, questioning our own and our clients' most basic assumptions about what is real and true. Our goal is certainly not to irritate ourselves or others, yet we may find that we do exactly that. At the same time, we may find ourselves the objects of others' anger, aggression, or even hatred. Moreover, we also want to help our clients work skillfully with anger and aggression. Patience as an awakened action helps us deal with these kinds of negativity.

PATIENCE: AN ANTIDOTE TO ANGER, HATRED, AND AGGRESSION

In this chapter we will examine the awakened action of patience, or forbearance, as the antidote to anger, aggression, and hatred. Because anger, aggression, and hatred are such difficult emotions to work with, and because the Buddhist way of working with them is quite different from that presented by many contemporary therapeutic approaches, there is much to say about awakened patience. I've chosen, therefore, to divide the discussion of this awakened action into two chapters: one on awakened patience itself and one on the specific practices that cultivate it. Then, before moving on to the fourth awakened action—and while we are already focused on working with the difficult emotions of anger, aggression, and hatred—I have included another chapter in this part of the book, chapter 17, which expands our exploration to three more Buddhist approaches to working with all challenging emotions.

For many of my students, the idea that anger needs an antidote is quite problematic. I have many students, as well as clients, who feel that they are only just discovering their own voices and that they are learning how to speak up for themselves as they never have before. Often this also means contacting the experience of anger for the first time. The last thing they want to do is have an antidote for it. Moreover, many of my students and clients insist that feeling anger on behalf of others who are oppressed and treated unjustly seems like an appropriate response as well. For Shantideva and for many modern Buddhist teachers, however, including the Dalai Lama, the problem of anger is regarded as the biggest obstacle to arousing bodhichitta and living a compassionate life.[1] They enumerate its many disadvantages as well as the benefits of patience. Let us look into all these perspectives on anger more deeply and see if these seemingly contradictory views about it are reconcilable.

From the Buddhist point of view, aggression, as we noted before, is the rejection of one's own or another's experience. It does not refer to simply being assertive or forceful. Rather, it is a pushing away of things as they are. That seems pretty clearly not something we would want to do. Even if we may choose to minimize our contact with some situation, first we need to see it for what it is. OK, that seems straightforward.

In his chapter on the awakened action of patience, Shantideva makes no distinction between hatred and anger, although we will make such a distinction in our discussion here. We can define hatred as the desire to harm or destroy an object as well as exaggerate its negative qualities.[2] There is nothing wrong with wanting to avoid this sort of hatred. It goes against the discipline of being present with what is happening and of seeking to cultivate the inherent sanity of ourselves and others.

What about anger, though? According to the Dalai Lama and others,[3] anger arises when we feel we have been treated unjustly or when we encounter something we do not like. It begins as a sense of dissatisfaction, discomfort, or unease. We embellish it further with internal narratives or by seeking confirmation from others. But, surely, recognizing injustice is not something for which we want to have an antidote, is it?

In his book *Healing Anger*, the Dalai Lama suggests that there can be "positive anger which can lead to altruistic action."[4] The difference is that this kind of anger, unlike hatred or negative kinds of anger, holds no ill will toward those with whom we are angry. It does not reject the person; it has no aggression in it. As we will see later, within anger, there is the seed of clarity, wisdom. If we can let go of any ill will, then we can, on the basis of such clarity, work on behalf of the welfare of beings. Needless to say, this requires a good deal of wisdom and compassion, and it may be beyond where many of us are in our development much of the time.

The Disadvantages of Anger

The anger we are looking at in this section is not the positive anger that the Dalai Lama described. Instead, we are looking at the far more common anger, aggression, and hatred that contain ill will. I will call them all "anger" here for simplicity's sake. According to Shantideva, there is nothing so destructive as anger. In the traditional Buddhist view, anger destroys our accumulated merit. The good karma that we have accrued by doing good deeds and working with our minds gets wiped out in an instant of rage. In the ordinary sense, we can see how this can be true in our day-to-day relationships with other people. After spending a long time building a trusting and intimate relationship with a good friend or client, for example, one angry explosion can require a lot of repair work. Words said in anger can be surprisingly precise and cutting. It may take quite a while to recover a sense of tranquillity, trust, and warmth with another person after such an experience. Sometimes, we never can repair the damage.

"You are so beautiful when you're angry." We may have heard these clichéd words used as a compliment, but the Buddhist view, by contrast, is that anger makes us ugly. Even if it doesn't make us physically ugly, it makes us unappealing. It is certainly not unusual for people to avoid someone whose anger is known to be easily set off. I have had clients who describe how they have angrily protested what they saw as unfair treatment from their work colleagues. Their points may have been completely accurate, yet they ultimately found themselves isolated.

Not only are we less attractive in our anger, we are also less likely to be happy or healthy. In contemporary language, we are likely to suffer the physical consequences of stress if we are dissatisfied with our experience and are cultivating anger. We may feel restless and uncomfortable. We may have trouble sleeping. The direct experience of anger is often unpleasant and painful, especially over time. The Dalai Lama points out that our inherent nature must be gentleness, as evidenced by the way we become ill from being agitated and stressed but not from being gentle and compassionate.[5]

As one of the three poisons, aggression is based on trying to maintain ego. The nature of aggression is to push away, or reject, experiences that threaten ego and its view of reality. Unlike a person with the equally confused poison of passion, a person who is caught up in aggression is actively pushing us away. With passion, people are trying to draw us closer. At least, they are right there to interact with. A person practicing aggression is simply less available.

Another important disadvantage of anger and aggression, from the Buddhist point of view, is that it clouds the mind, obscuring our clarity. We are likely to exercise poor judgment when we are angry. The other day I was ticked off by an anonymous note from a neighbor about barking dogs. I stomped around my kitchen in self-righteous irritation, putting together a few well-chosen words in my mind about how well-behaved my own dogs were, how unjust it was to accuse them of untimely barking, and how offended I was by receiving an anonymous note. I picked up the cutting board and set it down smartly on the counter. The knife sitting on the board flipped up and cut my finger. I imagine that we have all had such experiences. They can be moments that wake us up or opportunities to escalate our anger even higher.

An additional problem with anger is that it is so easy to grasp on to. We may find that we feel powerful and justified in raising our voices and overriding others' attempts to speak. Such certainty and power can feel really good to ego—at least, for a while. We tend to elaborate our story about how we are right, and we may drag in all kinds of irrelevant things. Causes and conditions come together to bring up old seeds of anger from the storehouse consciousness. We can really get going and lose touch with the present moment. This is the kind of situation in which we can create permanent damage to a relationship.

I suspect that every meditation practitioner has had the experience of the shocking contrast between what we can tolerate on the cushion and what happens when we get up and begin interacting with others. Sometimes, after even a very spacious meditation session, in which we find some peace of mind, we may find ourselves being irritable and testy with our housemates or family. It is definitely more difficult to maintain awareness and patience in relationships than by ourselves.

A worthwhile first step to explore with our clients is how useful their anger is. Is it true, as Shantideva suggests, that their anger causes them discomfort but does not actually lead to their getting what they want? What are the results of actions based on anger in their experience? In this way we are exploring the karmic cause and effect of their thoughts, emotions, and actions, as well as considering the possible disadvantages of anger.

Finally, out-of-control anger and aggression can lead to harm on both small and large scales. Feeling justified in one's aggression, narrowing down what one can clearly perceive, and mentally solidifying the negative qualities of the object of our anger lead not only to small conflicts but also to abuse, war, genocide, and every kind of oppression.

Surely, having a way to work with these difficult human experiences would be valuable.

What Is the Awakened Action of Patience?

The awakened action of patience is not the same as the sort of patience that many of us were taught growing up. That kind of patience implies waiting until what we want to happen finally occurs. It has a future orientation and suggests a period of dogged perseverance. "Be patient, Santa Claus will be here in just three more days."

In contrast, awakened patience is about being open to whatever we experience in the present moment. It is the practice of nonaggression. Nonaggression, as we have seen in our exploration of lovingkindness, is welcoming rather than rejecting our direct experience. It is not passivity or weakness. In fact, on the basis of being willing to be fully present with our experience, we may even choose to take quite forceful action. The key point in practicing this kind of patience or forbearance is letting go of our ego-referenced versions of how things should be and allowing ourselves instead to experience things as they actually are. This can mean, for example, fully tasting the intensity of anger for a few moments before deciding what we will do next. We want to respond appropriately and usefully, not reactively.

The Dalai Lama reminds us that we are the first ones to benefit from the practice of patience.[6] He cites a well-known verse from Shantideva's *Bodhicharyavatara:*

Why be unhappy about something
If it can be remedied?
And what is the use of being unhappy about something
If it cannot be remedied?[7]

When we struggle against how things actually are, we experience suffering. Just the other day I was waiting for my luggage to arrive at the airport after a long flight from Florida to Colorado. An announcement came over the loudspeaker: "Due to the number of very heavy bags, there will be a delay in the arrival of the luggage on carousel three. We apologize for any inconvenience." Harrumph. I felt discontented. I began to rehearse the small annoyances of the day: it was a bumpy flight; I had had to sit in the middle seat in my row; the food in the airport was dreadful. I was probably going to miss my bus! I turned to the couple next to me, ready to seek support for my irritation. Perhaps because I was working on this chapter, the verse I quote above from the *Bodhicharyavatara* suddenly popped up in my mind. Would my irritation and budding anger remedy the situation? Would it relieve my dissatisfaction? Clearly, it wouldn't. Hmmm. Maybe this was worth a try.

I began by repeating the verse to myself. *Why be unhappy about something if it can be remedied?* Next I thought about how it applied to the present situation. Yes, it was clear that my increasing agitation was not bringing any remedy to the delay of the luggage. No, there wasn't anything I could do that would help. My agitation was causing discomfort only to me. Instead, I could turn my attention to my direct experience. I could just feel however I was feeling and then see what happened. I noticed a tightening in my jaw, a narrowing of my focus to the information monitor over the carousel, an unsettled quality of energy in my body that was expressed in impatient foot-tapping. As I went toward these direct experiences, the irritation dissolved. I took a deep breath and breathed out a sigh. The bags did come late; happily, the bus, too, was late, so I made it with plenty of time to spare.

This minor inconvenience is a good example of one of Shantideva's suggestions about how to practice patience. He suggests that we begin by working with smaller annoyances and then work our way up to occasions that trigger more intense anger.

THE PROBLEM OF THERAPEUTIC AGGRESSION

An issue related to working with aggression—in this case our own as therapists—that has been identified by contemplative psychotherapy is "therapeutic aggression." This term is not, as it may seem to suggest, referring to the skillful or therapeutic use of aggression. From a Buddhist point of view, there is no skillful way to use aggression, the pushing away of experience. Instead, this term points to a common problem that arises for therapists: the desire to escape our own experience as we work with our clients. Through exchange, or simply in response to what clients bring to therapy, we often feel quite uncomfortable. "Therapeutic aggression" describes a reaction in which we try to get the client to be different or make a different decision, so that we can feel more comfortable. None of us really wants to do that, but it occurs often unless we have a way of tracking the subtleties of our experience.

My client Christina, whom we met in the chapter on compassion, met a new love interest. She happily described Roy as being, finally, someone whom she didn't need to take care of. Delighted with having broken out of her old pattern of having boyfriends that she tried to save, she listed his good qualities. He was self-aware and kind. He enjoyed all of the same things she did. She had never felt so comfortable and at home with someone so quickly before. He was an only child who did not work and was the heir to a sizable family fortune. I began to feel antsy. He sounded pretty spoiled. He was used to getting his own way. Couldn't she see that here was yet another man who would expect her to tend to his needs? I wanted to shout at her, "No! no! Watch out! It's the same thing all over again!" I was primed to make a therapeutically aggressive intervention, aimed at helping Christina see for herself that there was a potential problem with this guy. Of course, I would be doing this out of compassion. Right? Well, maybe that was part of it, but truthfully, I didn't want to have to go through it all again myself. I jumped to the conclusion that I was right about Roy. I was in the awkward position of seeing only his potential pathology, while Christina saw only his brilliant sanity.

When we are caught up in therapeutic aggression, we may offer unwanted advice, we may change the subject, or we may actually become subtly or overtly aggressive in pushing our clients toward our own agenda for them. In doing so, we undermine their wisdom. If we fall into this mistake a lot, and if our clients are smart, they will find new therapists.

In the next chapter we will take a closer look at specific ways to cultivate patience, any one of which could help us in dealing with the problem of aggression, therapeutic or otherwise.

16
practices in patience

As we have seen, the awakened action of patience is about working with anger, aggression, and hatred. In this chapter we will look at three ways of cultivating patience. In the next chapter we will look at working with all of the emotions, not just anger. The three practices that develop patience are (1) seeing how anger arises and not getting hooked by it; (2) being willing to bear our own discomfort; and (3) recognizing that pain is the source of anger.

SEEING HOW ANGER ARISES

The emphasis in this first way of developing patience is on understanding how anger arises and tracking it in our own experience. As we have already seen, anger begins with some smaller feeling of discontent. Something happens that we don't like or that feels unjust. Instead of simply seeing what is happening, we escalate our experience in several ways. First, we reference what we have seen to ego. So, not only has something unpleasant happened, but *I* don't like it. Then, we add a lot of thoughts that bolster and justify our viewpoint.

In my personal experience of anger, I have seen a particular pattern occur again and again. First, I may see something that is off: it may be something that is done incorrectly or that is harmful to me or another. That is to say, I have some sort of clear perception. Up to this point, it is not especially about *me*, and so it is still quite uncomplicated. Next, I have a familiar experience that I describe to myself as the *"yeah!"*

moment. At that moment I grab on to the experience with tenacity. I add more and more reasons why my feelings of something being wrong are justified and accurate. I become identified with my view, and it becomes increasingly difficult to have any perspective. I generate a great many thoughts, and I'm quite likely to raise my voice and begin complaining or blaming. The whole thing may feel quite juicy and alive. If I am angry with someone else and directing my words at that person, it is at this point that the possibility of backing down becomes remote. I lose my sense of a larger context, my compassion, and my clarity. I see, as I write this, that even in describing it, "compassion" becomes "my compassion" and "clarity" becomes "my clarity." That's it exactly. It is now all about me. I will now defend my position with self-righteous anger.

On the basis of mindfulness-awareness practice, I will, hopefully, learn to track this process earlier and earlier. I have learned to recognize that *"yeah!"* as a pivotal point. Sometimes I just override this recognition and allow the anger to escalate, but sometimes the recognition allows me to catch myself.

In working with clients, it is often helpful to track with them just how their anger builds. Many times, especially with perpetrators of domestic violence, for example, a person experiencing anger doesn't recognize smaller instances of discomfort before they are fully enraged. For such clients it is a helpful practice in mindfulness to assist them in learning to recognize the signs of anger as it develops. Then they are able to interrupt the process before they find themselves—seemingly without warning—completely consumed with anger and moving into violent behavior.

We might ask questions to help our clients recognize the physical, emotional, and mental experiences that form the early, middle, and later stages of their anger as it builds. What are the thoughts that accompany an angry outburst? What are the bodily experiences? Heat on the back of the neck? Tightening of the belly? What are the words that the person wants to say? What does the person actually want in the moment? What are their thoughts? A recovering alcoholic client told me an Alcoholics Anonymous term that captures one potent style of building anger. "Stinkin' thinkin'" is the collecting of resentments that build to the drinker's feeling justified in indulging his or her habit. Tracking the details of one's experience in this way is mindfulness practice. Based on it, clients are more free to choose how they want to act.

For example, my client Alison is very engaged in social causes. Among other things, she is active in working for the fair treatment of gay, lesbian, and transgendered people. Sometimes her frustration and impatience lead her to explode in anger at those who dismiss these issues. The result is that those people are pushed away. Finding a way to work with her anger before it pushes away the very people she wants to reach could help Alison be more effective in advocating for this cause that is so close to her heart.

It is also useful to examine more closely what kinds of situations lead to anger. The more we and our clients know about what triggers us, the less likely we are to be reactive. Knowing that being called a "bitch" will set her off, my client Marie did a few things to work with her reaction to that term of abuse. First, we looked into whether being called a bitch meant that she was one and whether defending herself made any sense. She realized that she didn't have to buy into someone else's label. She also practiced noticing her experience when her partner called her a bitch. As she did this, she remembered her father using this word with her mother, and she saw how it carried an extra charge for her. Finally, she found a way to remove that charge by playing with it. Alone in her car, she would amuse herself by bragging aloud about what a great bitch she was. In a sense, we could say she found the emptiness in the word. Looking into the dynamics of her relationship with her partner was, of course, another important part of our work, and Marie could identify the way that this present relationship repeated a familiar dynamic she had witnessed in her family of origin. Understanding that this old dynamic was embedded in the way her anger arises, and then taking conscious steps to let that safe and familiar anger go, allowed her to move forward more constructively into feeling uncertain, vulnerable, and tender.

BEING WILLING TO BEAR OUR DISCOMFORT

The second method of developing patience is simply experiencing what it is like to be uncomfortable. If we can tolerate, and even be curious about, the unease that leads to anger, we can short-circuit its arising. It is easier to practice this than it is to bring mindfulness to fully blown anger and rage. Once we are caught up in anger, it is quite difficult to bring mindfulness to it, though it is possible. This is one reason that Shantideva suggests that we start our practice in cultivating patience by applying it to small inconveniences.

This method, like our practice in examining how anger arises, emphasizes working with our own minds. We bring mindfulness and loving-kindness to the direct experience of discomfort, irritation, and anger as much as we can. For many clients, when they attend to their direct experience of anger, they discover other feelings. Often there is sadness and hurt. Like Marie, feeling angry may feel safer than feeling vulnerable. On the basis of the safety in the therapeutic relationship, clients can explore these scarier feelings. They may discover a shakiness, a quivery feeling, or sometimes just grief.

As for clients who find themselves already in the throes of intense anger, a practice that Thich Nhat Hanh teaches may be helpful.[1] He suggests that when we are angry we can do walking meditation while holding our anger as though it were a baby in our arms. As we walk, we breathe in, saying to ourselves, "I am feeling anger." Breathing out, we say something like, "Yes, this anger is still here." We continue walking and breathing and eventually our anger will settle down. The important point is that we are not rejecting our anger; to do so would be to practice still more aggression.

Some clients avoid bearing the discomfort of anger by cutting themselves off completely from experiencing it. Given the disadvantages of anger, we do not particularly want to help our clients plant more angry seeds in their storehouse consciousness. Thich Nhat Hahn discourages against trying to put clients in touch with anger by, for example, pounding pillows. (We did exactly that in my Gestalt training years ago.) Hitting pillows, he says, will not get rid of the anger. It may lead to physical exhaustion and the illusion that we have dissipated the anger, but it will plant more seeds of anger that can arise at a later time. "The seeds of anger are still there and may be stronger," he writes. "I don't think that in the moment that we hit the pillow, we are in touch with our anger. I don't think that we are even in touch with the pillow."[2]

At the same time, in the interest of not supporting ignorance, we do want to help our clients recognize what they are feeling. Many women learn as children that being angry is "not nice"; in some milieus that value being "ladylike," especially, little girls are not supposed to be angry or raise their voices.

More troubling is the ingrained defense against feeling their own anger that I sometimes see in abuse survivors, who often have learned that expressions of anger, no matter how small, could be dangerous, inviting verbal or physical violence. I have worked with many clients who firmly push away any indication of irritation, annoyance, or anger. They may become dissociated or smile and change the subject.

How can we resolve the dilemma of not wanting to feed anger or plant more seeds of suffering in the storehouse consciousness while at the same time wanting to help our clients reverse the habit of ignoring anger? In general, my own way of dealing with this conundrum is to bring curiosity to whatever my clients are experiencing. I often invite my clients to bring attention to their body experiences, especially if they are avoiding the present moment. Together we may notice what is happening right now as they are changing the subject, spacing out, or becoming distracted in some other way. Rather than pushing for what may "really" be going on "underneath" their present experience, I trust that what needs attention is right here, now. I have chosen not to employ methods whose goal is to heighten the experience of anger. Sometimes, however, in simply attending to the present moment, the experience of irritation or anger may arise, and I do not try to make it go away.

One woman whose father had been sexually abusive to her was afraid of staying home alone when her husband traveled on business, despite living in a home with a security alarm system and a large dog. As we brought attention to how she felt as she imagined being home, she touched into intense fear. The taste of that fear was one we both recognized as connected with her father. As she continued to explore her experience, she noticed that she felt tight and hot. She realized that she was actually quite angry with her father for still affecting her life. In the context of our connection, she allowed herself to feel the strength and confidence that accompanied the rising anger. She later reported that when she went home, she could summon that feeling of anger and strength when fear would arise. Instead of still being controlled by the legacy of her father's abuse, she felt like she was reclaiming her life.

RECOGNIZING THAT PAIN IS THE SOURCE OF ANGER

The third method of cultivating patience is especially directed toward working with others who are angry. There are several key points here. First, we understand that the cause of anger is pain, discomfort. Second, we realize that anger arises interdependently. Finally, as a result of this understanding, we refrain from meeting anger with anger.

If we understand that the anger that others are feeling begins with discomfort or being treated unfairly, we know that their anger arises from pain. When we can recognize their suffering, we can arouse compassion for them. As therapists, we often are privileged to be privy to this truth. As we come to know our clients' experiences, we can appreciate how pain leads to anger. Even if anger is only based on feeling insulted, this, in turn, is based on holding tightly to a false sense of self. Ego is already the experience of suffering. Those whose anger is based on being treated unjustly through pervasive abuse or oppression have suffered even more deeply. Our compassion naturally arises in response to such pain.

As we have already noted, it is challenging when aggression is directed at us. The temptation is to push back. Still, understanding the pain within anger can help us to not respond to anger with more anger. The desire to retaliate or to express our own sense of power will just escalate the situation. In the Buddhist view, aggression just leads to more aggression; it never removes aggression.

Shantideva describes how, based on interdependence and emptiness, it is foolish to become angry at someone who tries to harm us. Such people, he points out, are not actually in control of themselves. Instead, they are being controlled by their hatred. We should, logically, be angry with their hatred. Their harmfulness is the result of the coming together of many causes and conditions. In a famous passage, Shantideva says:

> If I become angry with the wielder
> Although I am actually harmed by his stick,
> Then since he too is secondary, being in turn incited by hatred,
> I should be angry with his hatred instead.[3]

Similarly, if we bring imagination and curiosity to the causes of a perpetrator's actions, we may discover that we cannot find a definite beginning point. As we know, most perpetrators were themselves abused. The history of abuse tends to go back generations. Where does the blame stop?

Instead of assigning blame, then, perhaps we can cut the cycle right here. Instead of generating more aggression, we can cultivate compassion, based on our understanding of the roots of aggression. Obviously, this does not mean condoning aggression or relieving others of responsibility for their behavior. Still, remembering the humanity of others and not objectifying them may help us as well as them.

Ed seemed stuck in his life. He wanted to go over and over the bad treatment he had received, beginning with his angry, alcoholic father and continuing with other men in positions of authority in his life. Unless I invited him to pay attention to something else, he would just retell the same stories again and again. Ed's father had been a frightening man to grow up with, and Ed hated him. He no longer went to his parents' home and he talked on the phone with his mother infrequently. He refused to talk to his father. Ed had a chip on his shoulder and saw unfair treatment coming even before it began. It seemed likely to me that his attitude tended to invite his bosses at work to deal with him as briskly as possible. This just made Ed feel even more insulted and angry.

Clearly there was some sane clarity in Ed's perception of his father as dangerous. Over time, we began to explore what it might have been like to grow up as his father had, the son of yet another alcoholic man, one given to explosions of violence. He began to see how his father's life was quite painful. He felt some sympathy for this man and came to see how both his own and his father's rage had pain at its base. Ed was not ready yet to speak to his father, but he softened a bit in his attitude both toward him and toward himself. As he became somewhat less brittle, he discovered that his current boss was not the ogre he had assumed him to be. "He's not such a bad guy," he said. And neither is Ed.

Having seen how awakened patience gives us some tools for working with anger, let's expand our investigation to some other techniques for working with other emotions.

17

our natural resources

working with emotions

As THERAPISTS we pay a great deal of attention to our own and our clients' emotions. I know that for many of my students and clients, emotions are regarded as somehow more "real" than other experiences. Emotions lose that special status from the Buddhist point of view, since they are understood to be both impermanent and empty. Yet, you may have noticed that the title of this chapter calls emotions "natural resources." So, what are we talking about? What are emotions from a Buddhist point of view?

In our discussion here, I would like to draw not just from the Mahayana teachings, as I have so far, but also from the Tibetan tantric tradition, whose presentation of emotions underlies how we teach them in the contemplative psychotherapy program at Naropa. Shantideva tends to present emotions simply as distractions, confusion, and certainly we do use emotions to support ego and its projections. In contrast, however, Chögyam Trungpa, drawing on the Tibetan tantric tradition, taught that within our emotions is wisdom. Emotions, he wrote, are like water colored with pigment.[1] They are made up of energy embellished with a story. The energy itself is not a problem; it is simply an expression of our basic awakened nature. Instead of simply experiencing this pure energy, though, we interpret it based on ego with its preferences, expectations, hopes, and fears. The energy is filtered through our confusion and is experienced as what we know as the emotions: including, although not limited to, anger, jealousy, pride, desire, and the sense of emotional paralysis we might call "stuckness."

As we noted in an example in the previous chapter, the basic energy of anger is simply clear perception. Then, we add a story based on what we like and don't like and come up with dissatisfaction that can escalate into anger. It is the ego-based stories that we add to the pure experience of clarity that create the confusion that leads us to unskillful, harmful actions.

There are three main ways that Buddhism teaches us to work with anger and the other colorful and intense experiences we call emotions. Each of them is useful, in varying situations. These three methods are (1) rejecting or boycotting, (2) applying an antidote, and (3) recognizing the wisdom in the emotion. The first two are more common methods found in different schools of Buddhism. The third one is a key practice in contemplative psychotherapy and is based on the tantric teachings mentioned above.

REJECTING OR BOYCOTTING EMOTIONS

Buddhism teaches a method that is seemingly the opposite of developing mindfulness and awareness. In the rejection method of working with emotions, we focus our attention on something other than the emotion. Then we do our best to keep our attention there—in essence, ignoring the emotion itself. It is not unlike counting to ten when we feel angry.

Since we can only pay attention to one thing at a time, putting our attention on some neutral object, like our breath, prevents us from either escalating our emotion or planting negative seeds in the storehouse consciousness. Moreover, it keeps us from harming ourselves or others. The drawback to this method is that it works only as long as we continue to concentrate on the neutral object. Nonetheless, it is sometimes an extremely useful approach.

This method is especially useful in working with anger that has already arisen. Asking a client to pay attention to his breath or to close his eyes and notice what he can hear can give him something else to do other than indulging his anger. While the client does this, his anger may begin to subside to a more manageable level.

Once, while I was on the telephone with her, Liz went into a long angry rant. I interrupted her and said that she was just feeding her anger. She stopped in surprise. Then she agreed that she was doing just that. "But what can I do with all this rage?" I suggested that she go for a walk for at least an hour and pay special attention to her feet as they hit the ground. She reported later that having something specific to do helped her not blow up at her kids and her husband as she usually did. She calmed down as she walked. It often takes a good hour for anger to settle down, and walking gave Liz the time for that to happen.

A similar approach is the mindful use of mindlessness practices, which we will take a look at in chapter 18.

APPLYING AN ANTIDOTE

The second method of working with emotions is to apply an antidote, a specific practice to counter the emotion. Unlike the first method, we are not ignoring the experience of the emotion. Still, we are trying to make it go away. We have already seen that rejoicing in the accomplishments of others is a specific antidote for jealousy. The method used by Marie, bragging and playing humorously with the epithet of "bitch," is another example of applying an antidote, in this case embracing that which she wanted to reject.

In the *Bodhicharyavatara*, Shantideva has a lengthy passage meant to be an antidote to craving and attachment.[2] As a way of dispelling the lustful feelings that his audience of monks might have, he describes in some detail how disgusting the innards of a living female body are, or worse, how revolting a woman's rotting corpse would be. Needless to say, my female students are often quite put off by this portion of the text! The idea, though, is that one ponders the unattractive qualities of whatever object one is feeling intensely drawn toward, as an antidote to desire.

A related practice that Shantideva advocates is remaining like a piece of wood.[3] That is, whenever we feel a difficult and strong emotion, we simply do not react or take action based on it. Instead, we just hold still as though we were a heavy log resting on the ground. This, too, can be quite useful, though difficult. Often when we are practicing sitting meditation, we may do something quite similar. We just let whatever is happening happen, and we don't react. Holding our anger like a baby, as described above, is another way of practicing this approach to emotions. This method differs from the boycotting method in that in this one we do actually feel our emotions, but we choose not to react to them.

RECOGNIZING THE WISDOM IN EMOTIONS

The third method is sometimes called "transmuting" the emotion. In this approach, we are quite specifically not trying to get rid of the emotion. Understanding that within emotion is wisdom, we are interested in tapping into our richness. It is important to note, however, that if we are unable to do this practice as described, then we are better off using one of the first two methods rather than planting negative seeds or harming anyone. It is a question of doing what is appropriate in the moment.

In this method we recognize that the nature of the emotion is energy and story. Furthermore, we recognize that the experience itself is empty of any true existence. Basically, the practice is to let go of grasping and directly experience the energy that has been co-opted by ego and its story lines. When we are able to simply experience the energy, it is already an expression of wisdom. Generally speaking, we have to be quite familiar with mindfulness and awareness as well as thoroughly acquainted with the experience of emptiness to be able to apply this approach. Nonetheless, knowing what wisdom may lie within different emotions can help us in recognizing our own and our clients' brilliant sanity.

As we have seen, according to these teachings, anger is the confused expression of clarity. Within pride or arrogance is the wisdom of equanimity. Sometimes, too, there is generosity. Instead of grasping on to a sense of ourselves as special, we wish that all beings can have whatever good things we have.

Without the reference point of ego, the basic energy of jealousy is what gets things done. Jealousy has tremendous momentum. If instead of directing that vitality toward the fear that we won't get what we want and that someone else will, we can let go of the story and discover the freed-up energy to benefit ourselves and others. Stuckness comes from solidifying the basic energy of openness and spaciousness. Instead of resting with uncertainty and not knowing, we "fill the space" with arbitrary thoughts and opinions in an attempt to escape the discomfort of, for example, feeling stupid. When, instead, we let go of our false certainty, we may discover a vast and open field of experience.

The emotion of desire is the confused attempt to possess someone or something. When we act upon this kind of desire we are trying to shore up our shaky egos. We want this thing or person to enhance our sense of ourselves as somehow worthy or desirable. As many of us have discovered painfully, other people generally do not like to feel possessed in this way. They tend to move away from us, not toward us. Instead, when we are able to let go of wanting to get something for ourselves, we discover the basic energy of loving-kindness or compassion: the wish to support the well-being of another. Not surprisingly, the wisdom within the emotions are the very things we've already discussed: spaciousness, clarity, equanimity, loving-kindness, compassion, and the energy to work for the benefit of others.

So, how do we begin the practice of recognizing the wisdom in emotions? Basically, the ability to recognize and let go of story lines is trained in our sitting meditation practice. As we release our grasping on to our experience, what remains is just our direct and nondual experience in the moment. Notice that we are not trying to achieve some kind of blank emptiness. As we have noted before, emptiness is not nothingness. As senior Buddhist teachers describe it, this "method" is actually not even a method or antidote: it is simply recognizing ultimate truth.

For those of us who do not usually rest in the direct experience of emptiness, we can use a slight variation of the touch and go technique, introduced in chapter 8, to move us in the direction of this nonmethod. Touching our experience and letting it go again helps us let go of the grasping on to the thoughts and false sense of self, which are the obstacles to directly experiencing the wisdom energy within emotions.

In this variation, each time we touch our experience, we can free up the object of our emotion. For example, if I am feeling irritated toward my colleagues for leaving some dirty dishes in the communal sink at school, I can recognize that this is *my* experience and own it as my own. I can let go of attaching my experience to them. Having done that, I go toward my experience and feel it fully, though momentarily, in my body and mind. This is similar to the awakened patience practice of bearing one's pain.

Next, letting go of my thoughts about the experience allows whatever texture and energy there may be present in the emotion to also be recognized. It is important to not fall into practicing "go and go." As always in practicing touch and go, we are not pushing our experience away. Instead, we are recognizing that it is already changing from moment to moment.

When I practice touch and go in this way, what generally happens for me is the discovery of a greater sense of freedom and space. As a result, I might have more clarity about how to proceed. Maybe I will choose to say something and maybe not, but I won't have to be simply reactive. What remains, according to this practice, is the "seed of virtue." That is, instead of planting more seeds of irritation and tightness, I will plant seeds of openness and presence.

WORKING WITH EMOTIONS
IN A THERAPEUTIC SETTING

My client Leigh worked as a social worker in a local agency dealing with cases of child abuse and neglect. One day she told me about her father who used to hit her as a child. She told me about that very matter-of-factly without any emotion. I was surprised and interested. As we explored Leigh's experience in the moment, she became increasingly aware of tension in her shoulders and arms as well as in her belly. She contacted a sense of fear and then anger. Leigh had learned to cut off these feelings as a child. Now she let herself feel the bodily experience of these emotions. At first, she directed her fear and anger at her dead father. (There was also some pain in recognizing that he was not simply the gentle man she had held in memory for many years.)

In later sessions, she brought more and more curiosity to her own direct experience of her emotions. As she stayed with them, an image arose. She felt like she was in the prow of a ship, sailing into dark waters. As her experience unfolded, she felt her anger transform into a sense of strength and resolve on behalf of all children who had been mistreated. Leigh recognized that her career choice had reflected wisdom without her even being aware of it. With renewed vigor, she continued her work with the children at her agency.

Charlene came into my office having just gotten off the phone with her boyfriend, Thomas. As she reported it, they had had a great week together and now Thomas was showing signs of pulling back. He was offering criticism of her, saying that she always made any disagreement about her own views and ignored what he was actually telling her about his own feelings. Charlene was devastated. How could he say such things about her! She had been entertaining fantasies of a long, happy life together. For many years she had longed for a family, and Thomas wanted one, too. How could he be throwing obstacles in the way?

To begin with, Charlene's comments were all about Thomas: about what he had done wrong and how it foretold a dismal future for their relationship. Then, however, she began to bring her attention to the direct experience of longing and fear that she was experiencing. She found this quite difficult to do. No sooner had she turned her attention to her own experience, then she would return to her litany of Thomas's problems. Still, she persevered and was surprised to see how many of her thoughts were about herself and how she wasn't worthy enough. Of course Thomas wouldn't want to be with her. As she moved more deeply into the feelings that accompanied these thoughts, she recognized them as a familiar sense of inadequacy and sadness. These, she saw, were her own.

As she allowed herself to feel these painful feelings, she had an insight. "He was right! I do change the subject and talk about myself. I did ignore what he said." Following that, she touched in to some empathy for Thomas. "Boy, it would be hard to be in a relationship with someone who did that." She was only a step away from turning that into another self-critical statement, but she caught it with a laugh.

"I'm about to do it again, aren't I?" Although this was probably just a glimpse on the road toward letting go of an old ego-story about herself, Charlene had a moment of transmuting her longing, sadness, and desire into compassion and empathy for both herself and Thomas. At the very least, she is more curious about her reactions to Thomas and eager to explore her own experience more.

Whichever method of working with emotions we employ, in our own lives or in our clinical work, the first step is being mindful, recognizing that we are having an emotional experience. Then, based on assessing in the moment what we can actually do, we choose to either distract ourselves, apply an antidote, or practice touch and go. If we can simply let go of grasping our own ego-stories and free up the wisdom within the emotion's energy, then, by all means, we do that. Choosing an appropriate method can be an expression of loving-kindness. It does us no good at all to try to apply a more "advanced" method than what we are able to do. As therapists, we can guide our clients in experimenting with these different methods as well.

18

exertion

the fourth of the awakened actions

THE FOURTH PARAMITA, *virya,* has been translated variously as energy, enthusiasm, endeavor, heroic perseverance, vigor, or exertion. It has to do with joyfully pursuing virtuous actions. This awakened action teaches how to get going and keep going. For many of our clients, this action is relevant to their issues of struggling with procrastination, feeling overwhelmed, or experiencing loss of heart. For therapists, the action of exertion or perseverance has a lot to do with working with some feelings similar to these, those known as burnout. In this chapter we will look at the obstacles to practicing exertion as well as Shantideva's suggestions for how to overcome them.

According to Shantideva:

> What is enthusiasm? It is finding joy in what is wholesome.
> Its opposing factors are explained
> As laziness, attraction to what is bad
> And despising oneself out of despondency.[1]

THREE COMMON OBSTACLES TO THE AWAKENED ACTION OF EXERTION

Sam described himself as feeling depressed. A bright man with a disarming sense of humor, he lived alone despite longing for an intimate partner. Long stuck in a job that barely made use of his abilities, he was deeply frustrated with himself. His confidence was low, and he didn't seem able to gather his energy and take the necessary steps to change his situation. Instead of addressing the changes he wished to make, he would become lost in computer games, drinking, or in worrying about the details of what he had said or done with friends or at work. Sam had a problem with exertion and showed all three of the obstacles to the joyful effort described by Shantideva.

The first obstacle is laziness, or indolence. Unlike the common understanding of laziness as a character flaw, laziness here refers to being attracted to a life of pleasure and ease. In contrast to the First Noble Truth, which teaches that we cannot avoid pain, the belief underlying laziness is that we can somehow find a pleasurable life by ignoring discomfort. Sam understood all too well that not taking steps to change his work situation, for example, was counterproductive. Yet, he continued to lose himself in surfing the Internet. The more he avoided the work issue, the more he experienced a sense of hopelessness about it ever changing.

Sam also displayed the second obstacle to exerting himself in a joyful way: attraction to what is bad. "Bad" here means that which leads to suffering. Being attracted to mindlessness practices like computer games and overindulging in alcohol are ways that Sam not only avoided his difficulties but also ways that he added to them. He sometimes exercised poor judgment following drinking. He had already been ticketed once for driving under the influence. Each time he engaged in these activities he planted more seeds of ignoring rather than of mindfulness, more seeds that were obstacles to the awakened action of exertion.

Finally, the third obstacle, despising oneself out of despondency, was perhaps Sam's biggest problem. Sam had a good deal of self-aggression about his failure to change his patterns. His sense of depression was directly related to feeling stuck and to the understanding that he was causing this suffering for himself. One particularly painful aspect of his self-aggression is common for many people struggling with procrastination: setting his goals so high that he could never reach them. He had suffered from this pattern of perfectionism since childhood. He felt discouraged about beginning anything new, since he believed that he could never do it well enough. It is no wonder that he felt stuck.

It is not that Sam lacked energy. He had plenty of energy, but he was directing much of it into his practices of worrying over small matters, playing on the computer, and seeking to distract himself through drinking.

THERAPIST BURNOUT: AN EXERTION PROBLEM

Burnout is a common difficulty for professional and nonprofessional helpers of all kinds. When we feel burnt out we feel like we are just plodding along without a sense of joy or inspiration. We feel tired, stuck, hopeless, irritable, and exhausted. We have lost touch with any sense of joyful exertion. Two hallmarks of burnout are frustration and disappointment. Both of these are related to wanting things to be different from how they actually are. Instead of practicing the patience of being present with our experience, in burnout we are often focused on future outcomes that don't come to pass. Sometimes professional helpers deal with extremely painful situations and find it very difficult to stay present with such suffering. This, too, leads to burnout.

Martha worked in a local social services agency that was responsible for investigating allegations of physical and sexual abuse of children. Sometimes she had to remove children from their homes. On the one hand, she was glad to be able to protect the children from further harm. On the other hand, the children were often frightened and angry, and in many cases they directed those feelings at Martha. It was challenging to be the object of their aggression as well as heartbreaking to exchange with their pain.

Martha often felt frustrated. She wished she had the power to effect real change for these children, and she was disappointed when the children were sometimes returned to their problematic homes by the courts. She often wondered if she was doing any good. Many days, she would drag herself home, collapse, and zone out in front of the television. The teachings on cultivating exertion, which we will turn to next, offer some suggestions for how Sam, Martha, and the rest of us could work with obstacles to joyful exertion as well as the experience of burnout.

THE FOUR SUPPORTS FOR OVERCOMING LAZINESS AND CULTIVATING EXERTION

Shantideva presents four supports for working with the obstacles to exertion: aspiration, steadfastness, joy, and rest.[2] They are useful in addressing all of the issues we've identified in this chapter, including burnout.

Aspiration

The first of the four supports, aspiration, suggests that we begin by remembering what our aspirations are. For the aspiring bodhisattva this means recalling bodhichitta, the desire to benefit beings who are suffering. It also includes reminding ourselves that developing the wisdom to benefit others can take a long time. We can use any of the methods we looked at in chapter 1 for arousing bodhichitta. Sometimes that's all we need to do in order to get ourselves moving again.

There are two other aspects of this support. The first, remembering the reality of death, is a traditional method of motivating ourselves to take action. Realizing that our time is limited, and that death can come at any time, encourages us to use the precious time that we have right now to do those things we value. My client Leah, for instance, came in a few days after her elderly next-door neighbor died. In addition to the genuine sadness she felt at his death, she was also aware of being grateful to him for reminding her that she did not have limitless time. She found that his death served to spur her toward the writing she had long wanted to do but had been putting off.

The other aspect of this support is remembering cause and effect, the teachings on karma. If we want to produce positive results, we need to take positive actions. One implication, then, is to put effort into positive actions. In working with clients, I am interested in what they do that benefits themselves and others. One client, who volunteered at the homeless shelter on Thanksgiving Day, reported that it was the first respite she had from the all-consuming anxiety she had been experiencing about her son who struggles with drug addiction. She saw that her actions were genuinely helpful and that she could have an effect on both her own state of mind and on the people to whom she was serving dinner.

As we saw in the four powers of confession, recognizing how cause and effect works also helps us take responsibility for the consequences of our actions, and that, in turn, can lead to refraining from negative actions. Seeing how his drinking caused him more problems helped Sam seek out an AA group and led to his practicing sobriety. Becoming interested in how she felt after mindlessly watching television helped Martha see that she didn't feel rested but instead felt even more useless.

Steadfastness

The second support for exertion is steadfastness, or firmness, and has to do with developing confidence. Unlike pride or self-inflation based on ego-stories, genuine confidence comes from a realistic sense of what is possible in the moment. Instead of berating ourselves, like Sam, for not achieving impossible goals, Shantideva suggests that we start by carefully examining the task we are proposing to undertake. If it is within our abilities, then he encourages us to do it thoroughly. Starting and giving up partway through undermines our confidence. This is an important point for many clients. Determining what can realistically be accomplished is a skill we can help our clients develop.

Leah offered that she really didn't know how to go about undertaking a large project like the writing she wanted to do. She had some insight into why this was so, including recognizing that she had never seen anyone model how to do it. We worked with how to begin, especially how to break down the project into manageable parts. She began by writing a short paragraph of what she wanted her writing to be about. By identifying this one small piece of work she could imagine doing, then doing it to completion, she began to build the confidence that she was able to complete things. Her previous style of starting and stopping had only added to her sense of discouragement and even depression.

Some of my clients call this taking "baby steps." A number of clients have chosen to give themselves this kind of homework between sessions. If they find that they cannot complete their work, we reexamine the assignment and find a way to make it more doable. One client wanted to put her condo on the market, but she felt overwhelmed by the project of "selling the house." Together we identified individual tasks to be done and set priorities about what needed to be done first. She began by giving herself the assignment of finding a realtor, and she followed through by researching three realtors on the Internet to see if one of them appealed to her. The following week, she made phone calls to arrange meetings with two of them. Piece by piece, step by step, she continued with the task, and as she did so, she felt a sense of accomplishment. She learned something, too, about how long it really takes to accomplish such a very large project.

Sometimes those of us who work in social service agencies have less choice about what we undertake. In such a situation, the best we may be able to do is to have a realistic outlook on what is possible. Then, we do what we can do. Burnout follows rapidly upon trying to do what we cannot. Anyone who has worked in an underfunded nonprofit setting knows what it is like to want to do more than one can. Confusing what we want to do with what it is actually possible to do leads to burnout. Instead, we can wholeheartedly make the effort to simply do what we can, staying present and not creating more suffering by wishing the situation were different. As noted in discussing patience: if the situation can be remedied, we do so; if it cannot, then getting upset will not help.

The best kind of confidence is unconditional. It is based on knowing that we can be present with any state of mind, not on having specific skills that we may very well lose as we age. Sitting practice helps us to develop this kind of unconditional openness.

Joy

The third support for overcoming laziness and cultivating exertion is joy. Traditionally, this support refers to joy in practicing the dharma, the teachings of the Buddha—but we don't need to be practicing Buddhists to appreciate having a way of working with our minds. In general, joy has to do with appreciating the goodness in ourselves, in others, and in our lives.

As therapists, we can help our clients to identify and appreciate the positive aspects of their lives. It is all too easy, of course, to focus on their problems. After all, people come to us not because they are feeling satisfied but because they are not. If we narrow our attention to only those areas in which they are unhappy, we do them a disservice. Instead, we can also notice the areas in which they are doing well, showing their brilliant sanity. In the context of this awakened action of exertion, we can recognize the positive actions they are pursuing and how these efforts benefit themselves and others. Sometimes all we can point to may be their steadiness in making and keeping their appointments with us, but this may still be important to acknowledge.

In general, we listen for the happiness and joy that may already be present. For many of my clients, living in Colorado, their delight in being in nature is a powerful support. Some clients hike, mountain bike, enter triathlons, or just sit back and enjoy the scenery. Other clients describe the joy they feel in friendships. I am always interested in the relationship my clients have with pets. Some of my clients ask to have Sunny, my little nine-pound dog, in their sessions. One woman, Mary, who is wary of intimacy and also says she doesn't like animals, has surprised herself by inviting Sunny to come into our sessions and even to sit on her lap. As she strokes Sunny's fur and sets boundaries with her about how much licking is acceptable, Mary lets go of her preoccupation with herself and comes into connection in the present moment.

Similarly, our mutual experiences of connection with our clients in sessions are a rich resource for cultivating joy and appreciation for us as well as our clients. We can also make use of the practices introduced in chapter 11 on the third immeasurable, joy.

Rest

The fourth and last support for developing exertion is rest, or moderation. For many people the idea of practicing exertion suggests working hard and not giving up until a goal is reached. This is a common approach in sports, for example, where we are exhorted to "just do it!" In contrast, the support of rest or moderation suggests that we do just the opposite. Instead of pushing through our resistance and fatigue, we need to pay attention to what we really need: a break, a rest, perhaps a vacation or a meditation retreat. Taking care of ourselves in this way can be practicing loving-kindness.

I have worked with a number of people over the years who work at their desks with their attention on their computers. Sometimes they lose track of their body experience. When they do get up they discover that their backs are sore, that their bladders are overly full, and their minds are tired. They may feel irritated or disgruntled. They have lost the balance between work and rest.

Taking a short break every so often actually gives us renewed energy. Remembering to rest may be challenging, and my clients have come up with creative ways of reminding themselves to bring attention to their experience in the present moment. One sets her cell phone alarm to ring every hour. Another person, who works at home, takes his dog outside for a few minutes every so often. If he forgets, the dog is sure to remind him.

Other ways of applying this support include actually resting, getting enough sleep, and refreshment. Exercise is very helpful, especially activities that bring body and mind together. Anything that brings us into the present moment, and cuts down the orientation on the future that contributes to discouragement and burnout, can be good.

Sometimes we need a bigger break, like going on vacation or going on retreat. It is important to make sure that vacations do not add to our sense of exhaustion rather than relieving it. Absurdly enough, many of us fall into the same speedy style of busyness that plagues us in town when we head to places of "rest."

For meditation practitioners, a very powerful form of rest is to go on a meditation retreat. There are many organizations that offer group retreats from a weekend to a month or more. Often including walking and sitting meditation in a silent, or nearly silent, setting, retreats have no equal in allowing us to slow down and rest the mind. Retreats may be done in a group, or they may be done alone. Solitary retreats can be quite hard work, since one is often spending much of the available time at tasks such as preparing one's food and taking care of one's cabin as well as practicing meditation, but I have never found anything else to compare with it in helping me reconnect with the warm and spacious mind of bodhichitta. Some retreat center resources are listed at the end of the book.

Working with the four supports of aspiration, steadfastness, joy, and rest gives us some practical ways of cultivating the awakened action of exertion.

19
meditation
the fifth of the awakened actions

THE AWAKENED ACTION of meditation (in Sanskrit, *dhyana* paramita) has to do with developing a steady mind. For therapists, this
action has to do with cultivating the ability to be unconditionally
present both with ourselves and with our clients. Beyond that, it has
to do with helping our clients develop mindfulness, which, along
with loving-kindness, is a key reference point in contemplative psychotherapy. In this chapter we will explore the use of both mindfulness and mindlessness practices as ways to help our clients bring more
mindfulness to their experience.

The word *meditation* gets used for many different practices. For
example, some practices are designed to help us relax or to cultivate
devotion to God. The awakened action of meditation is specifically
about developing stability, the ability to place our minds on something and keep it there. It is an antidote to having a wild and distracted
mind. Shantideva says that the person whose mind is distracted lives
"between the fangs" of the negative confusing emotions.[1] Learning
how to stabilize and settle the mind through mindfulness provides us
with the basis for exploring the nature of our suffering as well as developing the other qualities of brilliant sanity. If we can't keep our attention on our experience, we cannot change the habitual patterns that
lead to our suffering.

As contemplative therapists, the main way we can cultivate stability of mind is through our sitting practice. Although the mindfulness-
awareness meditation practice, introduced in chapter 8, cultivates

both the precise attention of mindfulness as well as the panoramic awareness of insight (vipashyana), we naturally begin by taming the wildness of our minds through increasing our mindfulness. Bringing our attention back again and again to posture and breath is mindfulness practice. Over time, and especially with the support of a personal meditation instructor, mindfulness-awareness practice opens out into the stability of mind that is a combination of mindfulness and awareness.

Shantideva encourages us to engage in retreat practice, away from the distractions of our ordinary lives, as a way to develop a stable mind. For many of us, this is a seeming luxury that our lives will not accommodate very often. Still, as we saw in the previous chapter, it is something we could seriously consider. We might even discover, if we try a short retreat, that it gives us a kind of support for our practice and our well-being that is more basic than luxurious.

THE FOUR FOUNDATIONS OF MINDFULNESS AND PSYCHOTHERAPY

When I first began to think about how to integrate the Buddhist teachings on mindfulness into my psychotherapy work, I was stumped. My first thought was that my clients themselves should just meditate. But not all of my clients were interested in sitting, and I had other reservations about teaching them to meditate, as noted in chapter 8. So I dropped that idea. Guided, however, by some suggestions from Dr. Edward M. Podvoll, the founding director of the contemplative psychotherapy program at Naropa, I became interested in both the formal and informal mindfulness practices that my clients already had.[2]

Some clients practiced formal contemplative disciplines like yoga and aikido; others had prayer practices. Talking with them about their experiences with these practices opened up some avenues for thinking about how to apply what they already knew about being present to other areas of their lives.

Other clients lacked these formal practices, but they engaged in many activities with the potential to become informal mindfulness practices. These included things like playing musical instruments and singing; engaging in physical activities like jogging, biking, and skiing; participating in team sports like softball, soccer, and basketball; or enjoying activities such as cooking, needlework, interior decorating, and gardening. The list was endless.

I became increasingly interested in what made an activity one that really cultivated mindfulness, and then at one point I came to the sudden realization that I was trying to reinvent the wheel. The Buddha had already figured it out.

An early teaching of the Buddha addresses the "four foundations of mindfulness." The four foundations of mindfulness are just what the name implies: four things on which we can build our mindfulness practice. As presented by Chögyam Trungpa, they are body, life, effort, and mind, and are explained below.[3] The more of these four foundations that are addressed in a particular activity, the better vehicle it is for developing mindfulness. For many clients, being in psychotherapy is actually their main mindfulness practice. The four foundations are all aspects of our sitting practice, but they also have their place in the therapeutic relationship. As therapists we can sometimes help our clients round out their own practices to include all four foundations.

The First Foundation: Body

A primary feature of any mindfulness practice is that it brings our attention to our experience of the body. In our often speedy culture, we can easily lose track of our bodily experience.

My client Arlene, for instance, is busily preparing to move from Colorado to another state. It is a big move for many reasons. In getting her present beloved home ready to go on the market, she is sorting through the accumulation of many years. She is feeling pressure to get things done quickly. In a recent session, it soon became apparent that her speediness was preventing her from being aware of her bodily experience. As she tuned into what she was feeling in her body, she realized first how exhausted she was. This had been revealing itself in short-temperedness. Then she saw that she had also cut herself off from a wide range of emotions: sadness, appreciation, anger, and fear.

As we have noted, emotions are energy, and we experience them through the body. If we are not aware of our bodies, we do not know what we are feeling. I have often seen that decisions made when we are not feeling embodied are subject to tremendous doubt. This is one reason why obsessional thinking, based as it is in the mind, and without the grounding effect of the body, rarely leads to wise choices.

An important teaching of this foundation is the difference between our idea of our body as opposed to our direct experience of it. Clients with eating disorders, for example, often have an exaggerated version of this, holding very distorted mental images of how they appear. Most of us have a version, albeit a much less extreme one, of the same kind of distortion. Instead of sensing whether we are hungry, for example, we might look at the clock. Rather than taking a rest, we push ourselves to complete a task. After our session, Arlene decided to go home and take the rest of the day off. She is considering slowing the whole moving process down.

In working with clients' informal practices, I am interested in their experience of their bodies while they engage in running, biking, practicing the piano, planting vegetables, whatever it is. For an informal practice to help cultivate mindfulness, it needs to support mindfulness of body. Walking while listening to one's iPod, or driving while talking on a cell phone, are activities that cultivate distraction, not mindfulness. In contrast, the walking practice for working with anger suggested by Thich Nhat Hanh, described in chapter 16, is a wonderful mindfulness practice. When we do that practice, we bring our attention to our feet as they hit the ground: the heel touching, the sole, the toes, the shift of weight from one foot to the next. We note the internal experience of anger, whatever that is.

My clients and I consider how to bring more attention to their bodily experience in their already existing practices. Together we become curious about exactly what they experience as they cook or iron or engage in sports. In addition, we often pay attention to their physical experiences in our sessions. In the Buddhist sitting practice, the technique for cultivating mindfulness of body is to pay attention to our breathing. Many clients find that attention to breathing, even in just an informal way, is a useful technique for grounding themselves in the present moment.

For some clients, it can be more helpful to pay attention to their sense perceptions than to their internal bodily experiences. For example, I worked with a client named Sean who easily got caught up in fears about his body. Sometimes we needed to explore those fears directly, but it was not a great way for him to settle his mind. Each time he brought his attention to his direct experience of body, he quickly began to come up with stories about how his painful kidney stones might return or how his migraines would probably prevent him from attending his sister's wedding. At times when I could see that Sean's mind was too agitated to pay attention to his experience, or when he was heightening his level of anxiety, I invited him instead to direct his attention outward to his sense perceptions. He would look around the room, at the objects on the wall, and at me. He would notice the sounds in the room: the fountain in the corner, the distant sound of children playing in the schoolyard down the street. He might feel how his body contacted the chair on which he sat and how his feet felt on the floor. Often, doing this would help him feel more present and less anxious. He was able to make use of this technique outside of sessions as well. Any client can be encouraged to develop mindfulness by bringing their attention to their sense perceptions in the course of everyday life: for example, noticing the texture of wool and corduroy while picking out one's clothes in the morning brings mindfulness to this ordinary task. Noting the colors of the autumn leaves and sounds of the traffic while biking, jogging, or walking lets these activities cultivate mindfulness and stabilize the mind in the present moment.

Of great importance for therapists, obviously, is our ability to be present in the moment with our clients. Coming back to our experience of body again and again is a primary practice for doing that. Not only does this help bring us into the present, it gives us the opportunity to notice what we are feeling. As therapists, an important source of information about what is going on, not only with ourselves but also with our clients, is our direct experience of our bodies. The way that we recognize exchange, as with all feelings, is through our bodies.

The Second Foundation: Life

Most presentations of the four foundations present mindfulness of feelings as the second foundation. In this version by Trungpa, we have a variation. Mindfulness of life refers not only to mindfulness of feelings but to being mindful of all of the textures of being alive. These textures include those things that we might judge as the least "spiritual." There is a sort of twist here. Instead of trying to get rid of "bad things," like our cravings and attachments, for example, we use them as the object of our mindfulness. As we have seen both in the teachings on working with emotions and also in the idea of spiritual materialism, trying to have better, more sacred or bodhisattva-like feelings just contributes to suffering; it is not a way to develop wisdom and compassion. Thus, the teachings on the second foundation are about being with our experience as it is.

The particular technique for this foundation is touch and go, which was introduced in chapter 8 as a useful technique for our meditation practice. Sometimes we can describe this technique to clients directly. More often, we introduce it indirectly, in the way in which we inquire about their experiences. We can invite our clients to notice what they are experiencing and also how their experience naturally changes. We do not need to push our clients to stay with experiences that have already shifted and changed. We may fear that if we don't insist that our clients "really get into" whatever experience is going on that they will never contact what they need to contact. If we have an understanding of emptiness and an appreciation of brilliant sanity, however, we can help our clients both touch their experience and allow it to dissolve as well. We can encourage clients to touch by going toward their bodily experience and then to let go by inviting them "back" into the room and into connection with us. Practicing this kind of alternation helps clients to titrate the intensity of strong emotions. This, in turn, helps them develop the confidence that they can handle their experience.

Perhaps because of my early Gestalt therapy training, I tend to be interested in the most obvious things. For example, when clients tell me that they are afraid to touch into a painful memory, I am likely to say something like, "OK, bring your attention to that fear. Just notice what that is like right now." I may wait to see what they say. Or I might ask in a bit, "What are you noticing now?" These simple queries suggest that whatever is arising is important enough to pay attention to and that, additionally, I don't expect that it will necessarily stay the same for very long.

For the therapist, touch and go is also a potent technique for working with intensity in the therapeutic encounter. It is especially helpful in working with exchange. It is the primary way that we can stay present and not become "lost in the exchange."[4] (In the next chapter we will look further into working with the challenges of exchange.)

The Third Foundation: Effort

This foundation is my personal favorite. The awakened action of exertion, presented in chapter 18, offers useful advice about how to develop and sustain effort. In this third of the four foundations, which also relates to effort, we have another sort of twist. Instead of creating effort, here we bring mindfulness to a naturally occurring kind of effort that all of us already manifest.

In our sitting meditation practice, we find that we lose track of ourselves again and again. We become lost in thoughts, emotions, or physical sensations. We forget where we are and what we're doing. We notice this because we keep abruptly returning to the present moment. If we observe closely, we will see that "we" don't bring ourselves back. Instead, we are just suddenly back again with no deliberate effort. This spontaneous phenomenon is what we become mindful of in the third foundation. It is affectionately known as the "gap." It is a gap in our ego-story line. For a brief moment, we are simply present, in a nondual way, and without a story. Very quickly, we come up with a new story, but for a moment there is no separate observer.

The technique associated with this foundation can be referred to with a phrase coined by Chögyam Trungpa, as the "abstract watcher."[5] The abstract watcher is really just another thought, not anything real as such. On the cushion, it is the thought that says "thinking." Thinking just occurred here. As we have noted, this labeling is not a judgment; it is a simple, neutral observation.

In therapy we can address both of these two aspects of the third foundation of mindfulness. First, we can help our clients to recognize times when they are simply present in the moment and not caught up in thought. Second, we can guide them in cultivating the ability to observe their own experience nonjudgmentally.

Many times clients will lose track of what they are saying and will ask me, "Where was I?" or "What was I saying?" Instead of telling them where they left off, I am more likely to express interest in what it is like right now to be experiencing a gap. I am curious about what it is like to have a moment of not knowing. I might even suggest, with some clients, that they might just enjoy this present moment, whatever it is. Most of the time, clients pick up their previous story or start a new one. I may try to explore with them to identify what just happened and what it felt like to find the story line again. Sometimes this is a reminder to clients about the difference between being present and being caught up in a story. More often than not, though, clients simply sail right over it.

For ourselves, too, when we are working with clients, when we lose the thread of our story, we can bring mindfulness to the gap. We can observe what we do with such moments. We can also model for our clients that not knowing what we're doing is not a cause for concern, but rather it may be an opportunity to just wake up in the present. Likewise, we can support the "abstract watcher" in our clients, encourage them in the activity of noticing what they are feeling, thinking, and sensing, and making these observations without self-judgment—which in turn helps them develop loving-kindness.

In asking about their informal practices, I help my clients to understand how they work with distraction. Do they give themselves a hard time? How? What do they actually do in such moments? How does the practice support noticing that they have returned to the present moment when they've been distracted?

Many of my clients are skiers and rock climbers. In both of these activities one's safety depends on the ability to drop distraction. I asked one client what she did when she was climbing a steep incline on Half Dome in Yosemite and began to run scary narratives about what would happen if she fell. "I came back to the feeling of my hands in my gloves. I noticed my breathing. I took a few moments to just feel my feet. I put the scary thoughts aside and paid attention to what was right in front of me." Instead of criticizing herself for being afraid, or evaluating herself for taking a minute or two to regroup, she just noticed what was happening, simply and mindfully. We were able to use that experience as a reference point in other situations where it was more challenging to let go of distracting thoughts.

With some other everyday activities, clients can make use of sense perceptions to notice that they are back in the present moment after being distracted. Rather than labeling "thinking," as we might do on the cushion, one client who is a good cook notices the aromas of the food. Another client, who gardens, takes a moment to notice the colors of the flowers and the feeling of the earth beneath her knees.

The Fourth Foundation: Mind

The key point in the fourth foundation, the foundation of mind, is recognizing the uniqueness of each moment. Especially in working with emotions, we have a tendency to assume that we are feeling the same thing that we've felt before. Instead, the foundation of mind directs us to the freshness of our experience. Each moment is "now," and it is followed by another new "now." As we saw in chapter 4, where we explored the Third Noble Truth, the cessation of suffering, it is only in the nowness of experience that we can connect with brilliant sanity. In our sitting practice, we practice this foundation by holding our minds "not too tight, not too loose."[6] That is, we neither attempt to "catch" nor hold on to each moment, nor do we hang back and just hope for the best.

As therapists, we can encourage our clients to notice the details of each moment. We can take care in how we ask about experience to not suggest that the same thing is happening now that has happened before. Once again, we are taking note of impermanence.

Another aspect of this foundation relates to the spaciousness and emptiness qualities of brilliant sanity. Steadiness is to be found in the vast openness of mind. Within that, all kinds of momentary experiences come and go. Each of these arisings happens just once and is followed by another equally distinct happening. Because of our meditation practice, we may be able to rest in that openness and bring it into the exchange with our client.

In a more ordinary sense, we can notice with our clients how each moment of experience has never happened before. We can point out, when it is helpful, how things have changed. Especially in working with clients who struggle with depression, we can help them to notice the inaccuracy of their belief that nothing has changed and never will. Alternatively, we can also work with clients to attend to the details of their current experiences of stuckness or despair. As we will see in chapter 21, on the sixth awakened action, deciding which avenue to pursue depends upon our wisdom in the moment. But regardless of the approach we take within each moment, we can use the fourth foundation to recognize the uniqueness of that moment and help our clients to bring the attitude of "neither too tight nor too loose" to their own moment-to-moment experience both in session with us and in their lives.

MINDLESSNESS PRACTICES

Our last topic in working with the awakened action of meditation is taking advantage of the many mindlessness practices in which both we and our clients engage. As the term suggests, mindlessness practices cultivate a state of mind that is without mindfulness and alertness. In the spirit of making use of everything and not pushing away any experience, contemplative psychotherapists use mindlessness practices in several ways with their clients. Moreover, we can help our clients recognize the sanity that resides within some of the mindlessness practices that they may have created for themselves. Many clients have developed such practices in order to escape intolerable feelings—for example, feelings that as children they could not possibly deal with. Survivors of abuse often have cultivated a variety of mindlessness practices that helped them in this way.

Disconnection Practices

Generally speaking, mindlessness practices desynchronize mind and body. The body is sitting here in the room, and the mind is off planning the day's activities or entertaining a juicy fantasy of life with a rock star. Or the body is here while the mind is spaced out or blank. Once we start looking, we will find an embarrassing abundance of mindlessness practices in our own lives: practices of body, speech, and also mind. Mindless body practices include things like working out while watching TV, eating while reading the newspaper, doing yoga while playing loud music, twiddling a lock of one's hair, or biting one's nails. We can also understand serious addictions and others disorders as mindlessness practices: alcoholism, drug addiction, eating disorders, and so on. They lead to states of mind that dampen the vividness of life. This may be exactly what their practitioners are seeking.

All of us, at some time or other, probably use speech to disconnect ourselves from our present experience. We may indulge in chattering on our cell phones while driving. Like Dustin Hoffman's character in the movie *Rain Man*, we may repeat memorized passages as a way to alleviate the anxiety of being present. We may misuse spiritual prayer and mantra practices to dull out our senses.

Finally, mindlessness practices can also happen just within the mind: obsessing about the future, fantasizing about a longed-for outcome to a business deal, dwelling on a pleasant memory. More painful, but just as mindless, is mentally reviewing a terrible event from the past. Many clients also have found ways to dissociate from their experience through the application of some kind of mental mindlessness practice. The result of all of these is to cut us off from our present experience.

Mindlessness practices have several hallmarks. First, the practitioner usually responds with irritation at being interrupted. We rarely appreciate the call back to the present moment when we are successfully engaged in a good mindlessness practice. Second, we lose touch with curiosity. We would rather not know what's happening. Third, as already noted, mindlessness creates a disconnection between body and mind. Fourth, and perhaps most important for helping professionals, we close ourselves off from our compassionate hearts. In fact, this may be exactly why we are indulging in a mindlessness practice: we wish to escape the pain of recognizing the suffering of ourselves or others.

The Mindful Use of Mindlessness

There are at least three ways that we can make use of the mindlessness practices that we have cultivated: using them as an object of mindfulness, replacing harmful practices with more benign ones, and temporarily reducing the intensity of emotional experiences.

I like to say that I collect mindlessness practices, so I always appreciate the ones my clients share with me. I think of nail-biting as a classic example, possibly because it has always been a mystery to me why anyone would want to bite their nails or cuticles. When I teach about making use of mindlessness practices, I sometimes ask for a nail-biting volunteer. Then, we demonstrate for the rest of the class how to use this practice as a support for mindfulness. Jake volunteered recently. Together we explored in great detail exactly how it was done. When does Jake choose to bite his nails? Sometimes it is when he feels anxious. Other times he discovers that he's already doing it without knowing when he started. How does he know where to begin? Apparently, any imperfection will draw the attention of his tongue and teeth. How does he know when he's done? Often it is when he feels a sharp pain from having torn a cuticle or bitten below the quick. What happens to his relationships with others while he's biting his nails? Well, it's a bit embarrassing, so he mostly does it when he's alone.

In bringing mindfulness to this practice, my student Jake has already begun to transform it. The next time he finds himself biting his nails, he will notice what he's doing in a new, more wakeful way. In the same way, we can walk our clients through this exercise, and teach them to use their own existing mindlessness practices to develop mindfulness—that is, by making the mindlessness an object of mindfulness.

The second approach to working with mindlessness practices is to use fairly harmless ones to replace more dangerous ones. Playing computer games is less problematic than abusing alcohol, for example. There is always some price to pay in indulging in a mindlessness practice; at the very least it plants seeds of more mindlessness. However, the very act of choosing to do one mindlessness practice instead of another is already sowing a bit of mindfulness. If we don't engage in mindlessness practices on purpose, we will still do them but with even less awareness.

The third way we can make use of mindlessness practices is in applying the first style of working with emotions: rejection. That is, we can concentrate on some activity to the exclusion of other possible objects of our attention as a way of calming down. Once again, we can look at the example of computer games. Once I needed to have an ultrasound examination done. It required that I drink a large quantity of water to fill my bladder first. I was told to do this at home before coming to the clinic. In order to divert my attention from the very unpleasant pressure I was feeling in my lower abdomen, I sat at my computer and played solitaire for nearly an hour until it was time to go for my exam. Whenever I stopped playing the game, I felt the pain more intensely.

For clients who are dealing with painful emotions, sometimes ones that are emerging into awareness for the first time, helping them find practices that let them take a break from the intensity is useful. Some of my clients choose to read mysteries or space out watching movies.

Most activities can be practiced in either a mindful or mindless manner. A client who rides his mountain bike over a rocky trail needs to apply mindfulness. At the same time, he may be using his bike-riding to block out the grief of a recent loss. Is his biking mindful or mindless? Our practices are often a combination of the two. The point is that we can bring mindfulness and curiosity to what we're doing, whatever its nature.

20
the body-speech-mind practice
for working with exchange

PRACTICING THE AWAKENED ACTION of meditation helps us to stay present with our clients. As we do that, we increasingly notice our experiences of exchange, which is, as we noted in chapter 7, our direct experience of another person. Working with clients and the suffering that they bring into therapy means that therapists and counselors often have painful experiences of exchange. Many times we find that we can touch into the exchange but cannot seem to let it go. We may feel stuck in the exchange or even haunted by particular clients and their pain. We have the resource of our mindfulness-awareness meditation practice, and we may also find that practicing the four immeasurables as well as tonglen is invaluable. Still, sometimes these are not enough. Body-speech-mind practice gives us another vehicle for exploring and releasing the emotional residue we may feel from our work with clients.

Body-speech-mind is a group contemplative supervision or consultation practice.[1] It was first presented in written form in 1987 by Bonnie Rabin and Robert Walker, though it had been used by members of the contemplative psychotherapy department for some years before that.[2] It makes use of the three traditional Tibetan Buddhist categories for understanding human experience: body, speech, and mind. In particular, it gives us an opportunity to recognize the obstacles we have to being present with our direct experience of our clients. As we allow ourselves to reconnect with whatever lies underneath those obstacles, we discover our awakened heart, bodhichitta. Seeing how we are holding back from connecting with ourselves and our clients is often enough, in itself, to reveal how we can move forward in the therapeutic relationship.

THE PRACTICE OF BODY-SPEECH-MIND

Body-speech-mind practice begins with having one person in the group as the presenter, and this person presents a client with whom they are having some difficulty or confusion. Occasionally, we might choose to present a client with whom the work is going really well to see if we are overlooking something, but generally, we choose a relationship that is overtly troubling in some way. Then, the presenter's task is to bring that client "into the room" by describing the person in great detail, as explained below. My experience has been that the group starts to exchange—in a fascinating and somewhat mysterious way—with both the presenter and with the client who is not actually there. The job of the rest of the group members is to track their individual experiences and to report them from time to time to the rest of the group. A guiding and useful principle of this exercise is for participants to assume that whatever arises for any of the group members, including the presenter, is somehow relevant to the presentation.

Another key principle is to stick to description, as opposed to interpretation, both in the presentation of the client and also in the reporting on our own experiences. This aspect of the practice can be particularly challenging for many of us whose training may have emphasized the ability to analyze and categorize behavior. In the body-speech-mind exercise, our emphasis is on the uniqueness of one particular client, although we may find it tempting to make connections to the similarities this client shares with others. So, for example, instead of beginning, as we might in a conventional case presentation, with "This is a thirty-two-year-old Caucasian male with major depression," we might start with "Paul is thirty-two and has dark brown hair."

Then we would go on to describe Paul in the three areas of body, speech, and mind. We avoid all psychological terminology and use ordinary language. Our goal is to remove the obstacles to connection, and conceptual categories can be a big one. We would describe Paul just as he is now, not how he used to be at some other point in his life. The examples given in the three sections about what a presenter might include are not meant to be exhaustive. There is no limit to what could be covered.

Body

Our first area is body. If we were presenting Paul, here we include the details of his appearance. We would include his age and his overall shape and size. We would note all the details that we could remember of his hair, eyes, shape of face, skin tone, ears, mouth, and teeth. No detail is considered insignificant. What are Paul's eyebrows like? Does he wear glasses? What do they look like? We would describe his form, height, muscle tone, and distribution of weight. We would comment on how he dresses, perhaps suggesting where we think he might buy his clothes. What colors does he wear? Are his clothes tidy and pressed? I like to include what a person carries, like a purse or backpack. Does Paul wear any jewelry? A watch? Does he wear a belt buckle with a logo on it? Anything that adds to the group's sense of what he looks like can be helpful.

What is Paul's relationship to his body? Does he recognize his physical experience? Or does he never mention it? What kind of posture does he have as he sits in a chair? Does he sprawl, sit up straight? Can the presenter show us? How does Paul move and walk? Again, can the presenter show us how Paul might walk in the door?

In the category of body, we also include how a person spends his or her time. Does Paul have a job? How else does he spend his time? Does he watch TV? Play softball? Go to bars at night? We include his means of transportation: A bike? A car? What kind of car? What kind of shape is the car in?

Another part of our description of Paul that falls into the category of body is his environment. Does Paul live in a condo, an apartment, a house? Is he homeless? If so, how does he manage? Who else does he live with? Is the place neat or messy? What's in the refrigerator? Does he cook? What does he eat? Where? Who are the important people in Paul's life? In addressing "body," we just note who these people are, since we will describe the qualities of his relationships when we take on the category of speech.

How is Paul's health? What physical limitations or special talents does he have? Does he smoke? What brand? Drink? Use drugs? Which ones? How much? We do not note specific psychological medications, since it is all too easy to then think we know a diagnosis with its attendant assumptions. Generally, then, body includes physical circumstances and the "givens" of the person's life.

Once we've presented body, if the group members haven't already done so, we might stop and check in with everyone, including the presenter. Again, we simply describe what we're noticing without interpreting it. We might say, "I'm feeling angry." Or, "I notice that I'm trembling and want to run out of the room." Or, "I'm totally distracted and having a hard time staying with what you're saying." Or, "I'm caught up with thoughts and trying to figure this guy out." We might also say, "I'm feeling bored" or "I'm not liking this client very much." The presenter just notes all these comments, which may or may not reflect the presenter's own experience of the client or their relationship.

Once when I introduced this practice to a particular workshop group, many of the group members felt spaced out and bored. Over the course of the presentation, many of them reported feeling impatient. They wanted something, anything, to happen. The presenter shared that this was how he felt with this client most of the time. He confessed that he often did introduce some technique so that something would occur. He realized that he did this to alleviate his own difficulty with staying present with his feelings. He became curious, along with the group, in what would happen if, instead of trying to escape his sense of boredom and impatience, he brought curiosity and mindfulness to his experience both in the presentation and later with his client.

Speech

In this section of the presentation, we focus on how the person being presented communicates. Included here are details of how the person speaks as well as information about relationships. An important part of our connections with others is how we work with emotions, so how the client experiences and expresses emotions (or not) is included as part of speech as well. We do not present here what the client says about why he or she feels a particular way, but we focus instead on how that person connects, or doesn't, with others. In this section we describe gestures and facial expressions. We can also include other forms of expression the client is involved in, including creative arts like painting, singing, or flower arranging.

If we were to present Paul's speech, we might begin with his voice: Does he sound like a tenor, a baritone, a bass? Does he modulate his voice or speak in more of a monotone? Is his voice soft, loud? Does his volume vary, and if so, when? Does his speech reflect the accent of any particular region or country? What kind of vocabulary does Paul use: Is it extensive and full of scientific words or does he use lots of imagery and metaphor? Does he struggle to find the right word or does he use a lot of less specific words? Can the presenter give us a sample by imitating Paul's speech?

What emotions does Paul describe feeling? Which ones does he express in sessions with the presenter? Are there emotions that Paul avoids? Or does Paul never mention emotions? How does Paul deal with emotional pain? Does he let himself feel it? Does he avoid people and situations that are painful?

What are the important relationships in Paul's life? Is he in contact with any family members? What is the nature of those relationships? It is more challenging to be descriptive in this section. We might say, for example, that Paul talks to his mother once a week. She lives in a nearby town, and he reports that he doesn't tell her anything that matters to him because he's afraid she will criticize him. He hasn't seen his father since childhood, and he is sad that he doesn't know how to contact him.

Does Paul have friends, colleagues, or neighbors who matter to him? Does he spend time with them? Or does he spend most of his time alone? Does he have a partner or spouse? Are there former partners who are still important to him? We include sexuality in speech: How does Paul describe his sexual orientation? Does he have one or more sexual partners? What is his relationship with his own sexuality? Is he comfortable with it? Does he enjoy sex? Does he never mention it?

A rich area to explore in the area of speech is the relationship between the presenter and the client. How does the presenter feel in Paul's presence? What feelings come up and what feelings never come up? When the presenter sees that Paul is scheduled to come in, what feelings arise? Is the presenter pleased, or does the presenter feel a bit of dread? How does Paul relate to the presenter? Does he smile and look at the presenter? Does he avoid eye contact and mumble in a soft voice? What does he call the presenter? Does he use the person's first name or does he use his or her title?

Group members can also ask questions. Some groups like to hold questions until after the presenter has finished with each section. Personally, I like to see what happens if we don't limit when questions may be brought up. The style in which questions arise about a particular client are also a source of information about the client and the presenter's relationship with him or her. For example, a student of mine, Polly, was presenting a client from her internship and said a few words and then stopped. After a pause, group members asked questions. This happened again and again. When we checked in after the body portion, the presenter said that she felt like she didn't have much to say. She felt a bit attacked and "interrogated" by the many questions brought up by the group members. She reflected that her client also offered only short answers to questions. Polly often found herself asking question after question in an attempt to get her client to say more, and she wondered if her client found this process as unpleasant as she did during the presentation.

It is not uncommon for a group to become quite caught up in the speech portion of the presentation, so it is important to make sure enough time is reserved for the rest of the practice. Once again, the group may choose to check in after the speech section.

Mind

The final section, mind, requires that we make inferences about the client. Unlike body and speech, which we can mostly observe directly or report what the client has told us, the characteristics of mind are mostly available to us only indirectly. Still, we do our best to describe what we notice, without trying to figure anything out. The presentation on mind includes the content of what matters to the client as well as any assumptions the client makes about the world, so it may include spiritual or religious beliefs and practices. Qualities of the mind such as intelligence, sense of humor, and the nature of awareness are also part of mind.

Continuing with Paul, the presenter might share with the group his sense of Paul's mind: Is it open and spacious, or is it crowded with details? Does Paul experience any distance between his thoughts and himself, or is he completely identified with his thoughts, taking them as "real"? Is he logical, or do his thoughts ramble and trail off? Can he stay focused, or is he easily distracted? Is Paul confident about his ability to use his mind, or does he believe that he is inadequate or stupid?

Does Paul engage in any formal or informal mindfulness practices? Does he have mindlessness practices? When does he practice either of these? Is he curious? About what? Does he identify himself with any particular religious group? What does Paul care about? What does he talk about? What does he shy away from talking about?

A common tool we sometimes use in the section addressing qualities of mind is to ask the presenter to compare the client's mind to a landscape. Is it vast and uninhabited like a desert under a pale sky? Is it colorful, noisy, and busy like a fiesta?

Group members may find that their feelings shift over the course of the presentation or that their feelings may become even more solid and fixed. Something that often happens, if the group has allowed enough time, is that some or all of the members may feel stuck at some point. If that happens, it is important simply to allow that experience to be as it is. Just as in the touch and go technique, letting ourselves fully feel whatever arises, including a sense of stuckness, can lead naturally to letting go.

Some groups like to take some time at the end to discuss how the presenter might proceed from here. Other groups find that they prefer to let the presentation speak for itself. They might choose to check in at the beginning of their next meeting to see what happened—or not. I have found that it is often best to follow the lead of the presenter on this question.

STARTING A BODY-SPEECH-MIND GROUP

A body-speech-mind group can be useful for professionals in many different helping fields. I have seen successful groups made up of teachers, therapists, and medical people, or some combination of these. It is beneficial if all of the members of a potential body-speech-mind group have some contemplative practice for working with their minds, but sometimes that is simply not available. People in the helping vocations often have developed a fair degree of mindfulness just through their work, so they may be well prepared to track their experience in a body-speech-mind group.

In my experience, groups that are made up of meditation practitioners do have a different quality to them. Having a daily practice of touching into and letting experience go provides a unique foundation both in doing psychotherapy and in working with exchange. Understanding that exchange happens because of emptiness and interdependence is a valuable insight that may come from our sitting meditation practice. Additionally, seeing thoughts as thoughts can also help us to let go when we are stuck. Recognizing the energy and sanity within emotions may also come from our meditation experience. All of these possible outcomes of sitting meditation affect the atmosphere and activities of a body-speech-mind group.

How large should a body-speech-mind group be? I have been a member of groups as large as nine members. The more members there are, the less often each person gets to be the presenter, but participating as a member even with minimal chances to present can be quite powerful and affect one's own work as well. Groups that can meet weekly are great, but I have also been in groups that meet as infrequently as once a month.

Body-speech-mind practice is usually practiced in groups, but I have seen it done, with good results, by pairs of people as well. My own peer consultant and I make use of it on a regular basis. I would encourage anyone to experiment with the form to adapt it for individual use, for example through writing or using a recording device of some kind.

Many groups choose to have a leader who keeps track of the process and the form. For new therapists, a body-speech-mind group can provide supervision if the group is led by a senior professional. Other groups, usually of more seasoned professionals, may choose to be leaderless or perhaps have a rotating facilitator. The leader or facilitator can help the group to stay with the form and also remind participants to describe rather than analyze. Most groups meet for an hour and a half or two hours.

Remember that all the group members' experiences are regarded as relevant to the client or the relationship of the client with the presenter, and in this light it is a practice of generosity to truthfully share whatever arises. The more open and honest group members can be with each other, the more information the presenter will gain about his or her own relationship with the client being presented. Ultimately, the most valuable aspect of this practice is the direct experience participants have in doing it.

21

wisdom

the sixth of the awakened actions

THE CONTEMPLATIVE psychotherapy program at Naropa has a logo that depicts a wheel at its center, which stands for the discipline of working with one's own mind: uncovering mindfulness, gentleness, and openness.[1] Surrounding the wheel is the outline of a leaf from a bodhi tree, like the one under which the Buddha attained enlightenment, which represents extending those qualities outward to others. An arch at the top of the logo spells out "Brilliant Sanity," which is, as we have seen, both the basis of our aspiration to help others and also what we hope to help our clients discover in themselves. For me, this logo represents compassionate action altogether.

The department also has a long-standing symbol—a sword, which we use in a number of ritual situations. For example, when the leadership of the program passes from one department chair to the next, there is a formal passing of the sword to the new chair. Holding the sword is regarded as holding the vision of the program. We also use the sword each year at our opening party—to cut the cake!

The sword is a traditional symbol of wisdom (in Sanskrit, *prajna*), the sixth awakened action. This awakened action is a sword that cuts through confusion, revealing the wisdom of emptiness. In addition, the sword also cuts its wielder. That is to say, it also severs any attachment to ourselves as a separate discoverer of emptiness. In this way, the sword symbolizes the nondual wisdom of discriminating awareness, which reveals things just as they are.

The logo of the Naropa psychology department and the sword

reflect two inseparable attributes of the bodhisattva, represented by the Sanskrit terms *upaya* and *prajna*. They are sometimes described as the two wings of a bird. Upaya, cultivated through the first five transcendent actions of generosity, discipline, patience, exertion, and meditation, is compassionate skillful action. Prajna, the sixth awakened action, is wisdom. As we noted earlier, without the clarity and insight of awakened wisdom, we cannot fully manifest the compassionate activity of the other awakened actions. As B. Alan Wallace put it, "Trying to be of service without wisdom is ineffective; trying to serve without compassion is dangerous."[2]

Awakened wisdom pierces through our confusion about what is genuine generosity and what is idiot compassion. Knowing what to cultivate and what to refrain from in the awakened action of discipline is shown by awakened wisdom. And so, too, with the other awakened actions: wisdom provides the clarity that allows us to express them fully.

Discriminating awareness wisdom is sometimes described as the eye that sees the truth of emptiness. For us as therapists, if we act compassionately but without an understanding of emptiness, our attempts to be of help to our clients can be misguided. Rather than addressing the underlying problem of ego, we are likely—usually with the best of intentions—to further support its solidity, thus adding to the suffering of those we aspire to help. The teachings on emptiness remind us that all phenomena are "empty" of any thoughts or solidified notions we might have about them, and that no one and no thing has true, independent existence. If we don't understand emptiness, we tend to base our actions on concepts that are not an accurate experience of reality. Skillful action cannot flow from such a mistaken understanding.

The awakened action of wisdom simply cannot be reduced to words; words cannot capture the direct experience of emptiness. Even Shantideva's chapter on wisdom does not tell us what emptiness is but, instead, focuses on refuting the positions of others who disagree with the teachings on emptiness. This leaves me, as a writer, with a difficulty: this chapter is meant to illuminate the idea that we cannot manifest the first five awakened actions, the skillful actions of the bodhisattva, without the sixth awakened action, wisdom. And yet, I can't capture the meaning of this wisdom in words. As I have wrestled with this problem, I find that my mind seems to short-circuit. I cannot find purchase anywhere; I am abruptly in space without a reference point. My conceptual mind just cannot get around the problem, cannot encompass it. In that short-circuit experience, however, there is a small glimpse of nonconceptual mind: the nondualistic knowing of awakened wisdom. In the blink of an eye, it is gone again, leaving me to ponder about what just happened and whether trying to describe it would be of any use to my readers.

We have seen hints of awakened wisdom in nearly all of the Buddhist teachings already presented in the book. The nondual wisdom aspect of bodhichitta is awakened wisdom. Recognizing nowness, glimpsing the possibility of freedom from suffering in the Third Noble Truth, is awakened wisdom, too. The clarity aspect of brilliant sanity is also awakened wisdom, as is the effortless effort we notice in the third foundation of mindfulness. On the one hand, awakened wisdom is an aspect of our very being, and it shows up again and again. On the other hand, stabilizing our experience of discriminating awareness wisdom is a fruitional aspect of the whole spiritual journey.

THREE FORMS OF AWAKENED WISDOM

As therapists, our ability to precisely discriminate what would be helpful to a particular client from what would not be helpful is obviously an important part of our work. Recognizing wisdom when it arises in our clients is another critical ability for us to develop. So, then, how do we uncover this inherent wisdom?

We can follow the format of what are known as "the three prajnas," or the three forms of awakened wisdom. This methodology can be applied to anything we would like to learn, and it is especially helpful in studying the notion of awakened wisdom. The three forms of awakened wisdom are hearing, contemplating, and meditating. We begin by simply hearing about what awakened wisdom is, to the extent that it can be put into words. Hearing includes not only listening, but also reading and studying. Then we contemplate. That is, we think about what we have heard, and we bring our critical intelligence to bear on it. Finally we meditate. In this context, to meditate means to put it into practice, first on the cushion and then in our lives.

In the hearing stage, we pay attention to the teachings on emptiness as well as the teachings on the attributes of awakened wisdom. We have already examined emptiness in chapter 6. It is important to remember that emptiness allows us to see things as they are. It is not a teaching about phenomena not existing at all. You could recall the example of my friend's big, colorful dahlias. You might, perhaps, choose to reread that chapter at this point.

In addition to the wisdom that completely penetrates the truth of emptiness, there is also what is known as mundane, or worldly, awakened wisdom. This kind of wisdom is knowing how things work, and it includes study in all the fields of knowledge. As therapists, we need to be knowledgeable about the fields of psychology and psychotherapy. We need to know the codes of ethics, the rules and laws that govern our work, and even the categories of the diagnostic manuals.

Another important aspect of mundane wisdom is being knowledgeable about the kind of suffering our clients encounter. This includes not only their inner pain but also the challenges they face in the world. As therapists we need to be multiculturally competent, for example, and recognize how society interdependently creates oppression and unequal opportunity. We can watch out for any tendency toward the kind of bypassing that tries to dismiss specific suffering by taking refuge in a mistaken understanding of emptiness.

I sometimes think of this ordinary level of wisdom as the ability to know the difference between the wheat and the chaff: this is edible and will nourish us; this is waste and should be composted.

In moving from hearing about awakened wisdom to contemplating it, as already noted, we take some time purposely to direct our thoughts into examining the topic. That is to say, again, we apply our critical intelligence. Do the teachings on awakened wisdom make sense? Do they match our own experiences? Are there parts that don't make sense to us? Can we examine these elements more deeply and reconcile the differences we find, or do we need to discard some of them? We can add contemplation to our formal meditation practice simply by setting aside some portion of our practice time for it. This is one of the reasons that we train our minds in stabilization practice. We cannot really contemplate very well if we can't keep our minds focused on the topic at hand.

If we have satisfied ourselves that the view of emptiness makes logical sense to us, we then can rest our minds and allow ourselves to recognize the absence of solid existence of self and phenomena. In that way we practice the third form of awakened wisdom: meditating. We cannot really deliberately experience awakened wisdom, but having heard about it and contemplated it, we are better prepared not to mistake conceptual mind for the awakened action of wisdom.

SOME CLINICAL IMPLICATIONS

Although there are some forms of psychotherapy that have been developed by therapists from the field of contemplative psychotherapy—for instance, the Windhorse Associates' holistic model of working with people suffering with extreme states of mind, or the approach of working with therapy groups as an interpersonal mindfulness practice—generally speaking, there aren't any "contemplative" therapy techniques as such.[3] Even the two examples just mentioned reflect more of an overall view than a set of specific techniques. Relating to each client as unique is, of course, what all of us aspire to do. Nonetheless, when we truly practice letting go of the concepts we have substituted for our direct experience of our clients, we find ourselves without the apparent security that a fixed way of working seems to give us.

I recall, with embarrassment, an early encounter I had with a client whom I referred to another therapist because she was not willing to go along with my insistence that we do Gestalt therapy in the very particular way that I understood it at that point. Looking back, I appreciate the wisdom she showed in resisting my therapeutic aggression.

Instead of taking refuge in a particular style of working, we bring as much wisdom as we can to meeting each client right where they are in this very moment. From the point of view of egolessness and emptiness, both we and our clients are changing all the time. Each time we meet, we are each different. With the eye of awakened wisdom we can recognize what is true in the present moment and respond appropriately.

What do we do, though, when we know that our awakened wisdom may still be in its infancy? As always, we do the best we can while being respectful of the subtlety and power of confusion, our own and our clients'. We can bring a dose of healthy skepticism to our thoughts about our clients. Recognizing that labels and other thoughts are essentially empty lets us use them skillfully. We do not have to reinvent psychological diagnoses, for example, but we can hold them lightly and be careful in how we use them. Used mindfully, they can give us a basis for communication.

We can extend this precision to listening to our clients' use of language as well. It is always helpful to ask clients what they mean by what they say. What do they mean by "depression"? Staying in bed? Crying? Feeling suicidal? Or do they just mean sad? When clients say they are bored, or lonely, or stuck, what do they mean? For that matter, what do they mean when they say that they are happy?

In a similar vein, we can choose to make use of all sorts of techniques. Instead of identifying ourselves as therapists who do a particular brand of therapy, we can apply techniques based on our insight into what will be genuinely helpful. Sometimes therapists describe themselves as "eclectic" when they mean that they do whatever comes to hand without precisely knowing why a specific technique might be helpful to a client in a particular moment. Choosing to employ a particular technique based on the insight of awakened wisdom is thus not the same thing.

As contemplative therapists, we remember that we are trying to help our clients on the path to brilliant sanity through cultivating their mindfulness, compassion, and wisdom. Based on our experience and understanding of our clients, we may choose to use techniques we have learned or we may choose to create something new on the spot. Awakened wisdom is the basis for playfulness and creativity, since it frees us from any fixed view. Perhaps a good example, given in chapter 14 on the awakened action of discipline, is when I told Lisa that I would continue to work with her but could no longer let her pay me.

Let's look at two areas in which transcendent discriminating awareness can help us: working with uncertainty and becoming free from personal history.

WORKING WITH UNCERTAINTY

An important aspect of bringing awakened wisdom to our clinical work has to do with how we deal with openness or uncertainty. As therapists, we often experience not knowing. Rather than seeing this as a problem or a sign of our incompetence, we can simply recognize the experience of space, of emptiness. Then, we can allow clarity, awakened wisdom, to arise however it does. Sometimes we have what seem like clear insights. Other times we remain confused for quite a while. Letting ourselves be confused can model for our clients that not knowing is an acceptable state of mind.

Clients are often in a situation of not knowing: how they feel, what they want, how to proceed. They are often in transition between a known situation and an unknown one. Being in transition is a common reason clients seek out therapy: they are about to graduate from college; they are deciding whether to stay with their partners; they have just lost a job; they are struggling with the imminent or recent death of a parent. Not only are these situations in which their habitual patterns and ego narratives are failing to work smoothly, they are also opportunities to recognize the openness and freedom of letting go of a false sense of oneself.

In contemplative psychotherapy, we do our best to support this process while also helping clients to have some loving-kindness. There is no recipe that will always work. Working with not knowing is always a bit of a balancing act: bringing enough mindfulness, openness, and loving-kindness to one's experience so that one becomes neither overwhelmed nor stuck. Still, whatever happens, we just bring more curiosity and warmth to it. We can, from that point of view, let go of having to be right or fearing to get it wrong. As in sitting practice, we can always take a fresh start and begin again in the moment. And when we do so, we teach our clients that they can, too.

In helping clients to make choices, we help them practice not taking sides. I have noticed that personally I easily take sides, grasping on to one or another version of reality that supports some version of myself. To offer a literal example: when I enter a room in which my husband is watching a basketball game, I go from my initial openness, even indifference, about the game to caring intensely about some team that I have never even heard of before. I will latch on to some detail or other, become a fan of one team and not the other, and create the cause of suffering if "my" team loses.

My client Darlene was a young woman in her late twenties who wanted to make some decisions about her career path. Instead of looking into possibilities though, she tended to shut down and get lost in mindlessness. She had a low-paying job driving a shuttle bus around the local college campus. She literally spent her time going in circles. As we worked together with helping her tolerate the direct experience of not knowing, she experimented with longer and longer periods of allowing her confusion to be just whatever it was. It took a while, and required some exploration of the beliefs and feelings that arose when she let go of her habitual mindlessness, but at some point she had a clear sense of what she wanted to do. Darlene applied to law schools and ended up working as a legal aid attorney. Permitting herself to experience space, and not filling it with distraction, allowed Darlene to have moments of insight that led to a decision that felt right to her.

Sometimes encouraging clients to "live with the question" rather than urging them to reach a conclusion can be a big relief to them. Kelly had had two miscarriages and wasn't sure whether she wanted to try to get pregnant again. She had wholeheartedly wanted to become pregnant the first two times. Since then, however, she had become intensely ambivalent. She developed a practice of tracking her mind and heart about this important question. She would note out loud, several times a day, just how she felt about getting pregnant.

"Right now I'm really wanting to have a baby. I can imagine holding her in my arms, and I feel very loving."

"Now I'm thinking that I don't want to be the kind of mother who doesn't have time for her child. I want to be a good mother."

"I don't want to stop working. I love what I do, and I'm just getting good at it."

Going toward her confusion and letting herself take her time eventually brought Kelly to the realization that she actually did not want to have a baby at this time. It wasn't a matter of pros and cons or even of which side got more airtime in her speaking aloud. At some point, she finally just knew. She felt some sadness and grief, but she was clear about her decision. Part of what she had to let go of was her view of herself as someone who wanted to be a mother. She also identified being influenced by a strong cultural message that to be a "real" woman she needed to be a mom. The potential of motherhood had long formed part of her self-definition, and losing this identity was one of the things she grieved. She found, to her surprise, that she had tremendous energy available for other things once she had made her choice.

BECOMING FREE FROM PERSONAL HISTORY

One way that we and our clients miss out on the brilliant sanity available in the nowness of the present moment is by clinging to the past. It is not that we need to forget about the past and certainly not that we should avoid talking about it in therapy. Hanging on to what happened in the past, though, is a problem in a couple of ways. First, clinging is, in itself, a cause of suffering. It perpetuates a belief in an unchanging self. And second, to the extent that we hold on to a no-longer-existent past, we are not available for the unfolding present. We miss our lives when we cling to the past.

Not long ago, I attended a professional conference in which we spent a good chunk of time meeting in process groups. The group of which I was a member was composed of senior clinicians from a variety of backgrounds. This was a group of bright, insightful, and courageous people, but they had not been exposed to the teachings on emptiness. I was surprised by the extent to which many of them presented themselves in terms of their childhoods and their early familial relationships. They described their present behavior as not just stemming from, but of repeating, those early patterns. "I am still trying to please my father," one might say. Or, "My brother was always given preferential treatment, so I don't expect the leader is going to pay attention to me."

Of course, the patterns we learn in childhood have a powerful influence on us, and much fruitful time may be spent in therapy in seeing how those patterns are still occurring. But, awakened wisdom and the teachings on emptiness direct us to seeing how both the memories themselves and the selves playing them out are neither solid nor permanent. Instead of replanting those seeds again and again, we can learn from memories and also let them go.

Marcy's father had sexually abused her and her siblings. When I first met her she had cut off all contact with him and with her mother. Her mother disbelieved her, as did one of her sisters. At some point the opportunity arose to attend the other sister's wedding. She wanted to go, but she did not want to interact with either of her parents. She carefully made arrangements so that she could enter the church just before the service and then leave just as it ended. She would forego the reception. She followed her plan, and when she came to see me for our next session, she reported how her father had looked so much older.

In our talking together, she saw how the man who had so devastatingly hurt her no longer existed. As her father aged and became ill with cancer, she decided to go visit him. Without bringing up the abuse, she simply met him as he was. As he neared death, she was surprised to feel some compassion for him. In a session with me right after he died, she struggled to find language for how she felt. She wasn't just sad; she also felt soft and open. Perhaps, I suggested, she felt forgiveness? Yes, that did describe it, but was that allowed? Could she feel that?

"Do you?" I asked. Yes, that is just how she felt. She did not forget what he had done or condone it, but over time she had found some freedom in letting go of her self-identification as an abuse survivor. She didn't need to pick up that burden again. It could be allowed to dissolve into its empty nature.

A metaphor that I often use with people who are grieving is that they are like hosts whose guests are getting ready to depart. When guests arrive, we give them our best: delicious food, tasty drinks, lovely music, and a comfortable seat. We enjoy their company and feel enriched by their presence. Then, when it is time for them to leave, we give them their coats and walk them to the door. We wish them a good journey and don't hang on to their coat sleeves as they go out the door. We appreciate their visit and remember them, but we allow them to go. We can have the same attitude toward our own pasts: we can appreciate them, learn from them, and also let them go.

As we become seasoned in the field of psychotherapy, we rely increasingly on our intuitive sense of what is happening with our clients. One aspect of that is, of course, simply our accumulated experience. We are less often shocked or surprised by what clients may bring to us. We may also have more confidence that we can be present with our own and our clients' difficult experiences, since we have done so before. However, another aspect of our ability to rely on our intuition is the development of the wisdom of discriminating awareness. As we become increasingly willing not to know and to allow ourselves to relax into a sense of openness, not supported by ego and its narratives, we discover that often we do actually know and deeply understand what is happening. We have begun to tap into our inherent, awakened wisdom.

22
dedicating the merit

A FINAL PRACTICE in the Mahayana path is known as "dedicating the merit." Instead of thinking about all of the good karmic seeds that they are planting in the storehouse consciousness, bodhisattvas give away all of the good karma or merit that they have accumulated for the benefit of others. It is like cooking a meal of all of our favorite foods and inviting everyone we know to a great feast. Then, as the hosts, we serve everyone the delicious food and don't keep aside even a small dish of it for ourselves. It is not that we are depriving ourselves, it is that we are that generous and openhearted when we are in touch with bodhichitta. Paradoxically, by giving away the merit we have accumulated, we plant the seeds of the very same bodhichitta that we aspire to be further cultivated in ourselves.

Aspiring bodhisattvas emulate the fully awakened bodhisattvas, when they perform the Mahayana practices like the ones described in this book, by dividing their formal practice sessions into three parts. We begin by arousing bodhichitta. Then we engage in our main practice, which might include mindfulness-awareness, tonglen, the four immeasurables, or other contemplations. Finally, we conclude, or seal, our practice by dedicating whatever merit we have gathered to all beings, with the wish that they might be freed from suffering and realize their own awakened nature. In that way, bodhichitta pervades our practice at the beginning, in the middle, and at the end.

Often dedicating the merit is done by reciting a formal prayer, but it could also simply be an attitude and a wish we mindfully hold at the end of our practice. However we undertake it, the goal of dedicating the merit is to further let go of any selfish motivation.

As therapists and counselors, we could have a similar attitude toward our work with our clients. In the same way that we might start our meditation practice by arousing bodhichitta, we could start our work with each client by arousing the heartfelt desire to be of benefit that led us to become therapists and counselors in the first place. As we have noted before, our work with clients is similar to spiritual practice, because in both activities we aspire to develop and manifest wisdom and compassion. Acting on this idea, we could decide that at the close of each session, quietly to ourselves, we will dedicate the merit of our work to the benefit of that client. We can simply use whatever words and images seem appropriate to us on the spot. Moreover, we can hold the wish that our clients will develop the strengths and qualities that will allow them to manage on their own, without our help.

One of my students, who was doing her internship working with adolescent girls, came up with what I think of as a delightful dedication practice. At the end of the day, she sat once more in her chair and imagined each client she had worked with that day, one after the other, sitting in the chair opposite her. With each one, she imagined offering the client whatever she needed. She also would let go of anything she felt had been a mistake in her own work and resolve to do what she could to be helpful the next time they met. Then she would say, "Good night, for now." In that way, she not only practiced generosity, she also cultivated some loving-kindness for herself and let go of the day's work before going home.

When our work is difficult, or when we don't see any improvement in our clients, we can still dedicate the merit. If we have not managed to do anything else for our clients, we have done this: we have offered to them the good seeds, the good karma, that are the result of our own good intentions. This can also help us let go of our expectations and desires to accomplish what we have not or cannot. In bringing us back once again to our pure intention, bodhichitta, dedicating the merit can remind us at the end of our work of the intentions with which we began it.

Shantideva ends the *Bodhicharyavatara* with an elaborate dedication of merit. Below are a few of those verses. As you read these verses, if you like, you can join Shantideva in dedicating the merit of having engaged with these teachings for the benefit of your clients or other beings. I, too, make that wish.

> May all beings everywhere
> Plagued with sufferings of body and mind
> Obtain an ocean of happiness and joy
> By virtue of my merits.[1]

> May no living creature ever suffer,
> Commit evil or ever fall ill.
> May no one be afraid or belittled,
> Or their minds ever be depressed.[2]

> For as long as space endures
> And for as long as living beings remain,
> Until then may I too abide
> To dispel the misery of the world.[3]

notes

INTRODUCTION

1. Several translations of Shantideva's *Bodhicharyavatara* are available in English. This book uses *A Guide to the Bodhisattva's Way of Life,* trans. Stephen Batchelor (Dharamsala, India: Library of Tibetan Works and Archives, 1979). Please note also that while *The Courage to Be Present* has been inspired in part by Shantideva's *Bodhicharyavatara,* it is not a commentary on that text. Interested readers will find three such commentaries listed in the Resources section at the end of the book. All verses from the *Bodhicharyavatara* are used by permission and are taken from *A Guide to the Bodhisattva's Way of Life,* translated by Stephen Batchelor and published by the Library of Tibetan Works & Archives, Dharamsala H.P. 176215 (India).

PART ONE

1. Shantideva, *A Guide to the Bodhisattva's Way of Life,* trans. Stephen Batchelor (Dharamsala, India: Library of Tibetan Works and Archives, 1979), verse 28. Batchelor translated *bodhichitta* as "An Awakening Mind." I have chosen to use the original term, *bodhichitta,* in this passage instead.

CHAPTER 1
The Awakened Heart of the Bodhisattva

1. Although many people confuse the Hinayana teachings with the Theravadin Buddhist tradition, which is still practiced in Southeast Asia as well as in the West, a contemporary Tibetan Buddhist teacher, Traleg Kyabgon, has explained that *Hinayana* is a term created by Mahayana practitioners to refer to a school of Indian Buddhism no longer in existence, and

not to the oldest still-existing Buddhist school, the Theravadin. See Traleg Kyabgon, *Mind at Ease* (Boston: Shambhala Publications, 2004), 12.

2. Chögyam Trungpa, *The Heart of the Buddha*, ed. Judith L. Lief (Boston: Shambhala Publications, 1991), 108–31.

CHAPTER 2
Acknowledging Suffering

1. Charlotte Joko Beck, *Everyday Zen: Love and Work*, ed. Steve Smith (San Francisco: HarperSanFrancisco, 1989), 105.

CHAPTER 3
Why Are We So Confused?

1. Thich Nhat Hanh, *Being Peace*, ed. Arnold Kotler (Berkeley: Parallax Press, 1987), 87.

2. Shantideva, *A Guide to the Bodhisattva's Way of Life*, trans. Stephen Batchelor (Dharamsala, India: Library of Tibetan Works and Archives, 1979), 125.

3. Thich Nhat Hanh, "Planting Good Seeds," *Journal of Contemplative Psychotherapy* 7 (1990): 97–107.

CHAPTER 5
The Path

1. Thich Nhat Hanh, *The Practice of Mindfulness in Psychotherapy 1* and *2* (Boulder, Colo.: Sounds True Recordings, 1990), audiocassettes.

2. Chögyam Trungpa, *Cutting through Spiritual Materialism*, eds. John Baker and Marvin Casper (Boston: Shambhala Publications, 1973), 13–22.

3. Frederick Perls, Roger Hefferline, and Paul Goodman, *Gestalt Therapy: Excitement and Growth in the Human Personality* (Gouldsboro, Maine: Gestalt Journal Press, 1994), 64. This basic text on Gestalt therapy first appeared in 1951.

CHAPTER 6
Emptiness Is Not Nothingness

1. Khenpo Tsültrim Gyamtso, *Progressive Stages of Meditation on Emptiness*, 2nd ed., trans. Shenpen Hookham (Oxford, U.K.: Longchen Foundation, 1988).

2. John Welwood, *Toward a Psychology of Awakening: Buddhism, Psychotherapy, and the Path of Personal and Spiritual Transformation* (Boston: Shambhala Publications, 2000), 207.

CHAPTER 7
May I Be a Bridge, a Ship, or a . . . Psychotherapist?
1. Chögyam Trungpa originally designed a logo, featuring the term "brilliant sanity," for the cover of the *Naropa Institute Journal of Psychology* 1 (1980).

CHAPTER 8
Meditation
1. Chögyam Trungpa, *The Sanity We Are Born With: A Buddhist Approach to Psychology*, ed. Carolyn Rose Gimian (Boston: Shambhala Publications, 2005), 28.

CHAPTER 9
The First Immeasurable
1. Chögyam Trungpa, *The Sanity We Are Born With: A Buddhist Approach to Psychology*, ed. Carolyn Rose Gimian (Boston: Shambhala Publications, 2005), 146.
2. B. Alan Wallace, *The Four Immeasurables: Cultivating a Boundless Heart*, ed. Zara Houshmand, 2nd ed. (Ithaca, N.Y.: Snow Lion, 2004), 88–89.

CHAPTER 10
The Second Immeasurable
1. Chögyam Trungpa, *Cutting Through Spiritual Materialism*, eds. John Baker and Marvin Casper (Boston: Shambhala Publications, 1973), 97.

CHAPTER 11
The Third Immeasurable
1. Pema Chödrön, *The Places That Scare You: A Guide to Fearlessness in Difficult Times* (Boston: Shambhala Publications, 2001), 62.
2. B. Alan Wallace, *The Four Immeasurables: Cultivating a Boundless Heart*, ed. Zara Houshmand, 2nd ed. (Ithaca, N.Y.: Snow Lion, 2004), 144.

CHAPTER 12
The Fourth Immeasurable
1. B. Alan Wallace, *The Four Immeasurables: Cultivating a Boundless Heart*, ed. Zara Houshmand, 2nd ed. (Ithaca, N.Y.: Snow Lion, 2004), 161.
2. Rumi, *The Essential Rumi*, trans. Coleman Barks and John Moyne (San Francisco: HarperSanFrancisco, 1995), 109.
3. Thich Nhat Hanh, *Being Peace*, ed. Arnold Kotler (Berkeley: Parallax Press, 1987), 62–64.

4. John Stevens, "Introduction," *One Robe, One Bowl: The Zen Poetry of Ryo-kan,* trans. John Stevens, 1st ed. (New York: Weatherhill, 1984), 12, 14.

5. Judith Simmer-Brown, *Dakini's Warm Breath: The Feminine Principle in Tibetan Buddhism* (Boston: Shambhala Publications, 2002), 197, 199.

6. For a more thorough discussion of these differences, see chapters 11 through 13 in Harvey Aronson, *Buddhist Practice on Western Ground: Reconciling Eastern Ideals and Western Psychology* (Boston: Shambhala Publications, 2004), 151–83.

7. See Wallace, *The Four Immeasurables,* 155, and Pema Chödrön, *No Time to Lose: A Timely Guide to the Way of the Bodhisattva* (Boston: Shambhala Publications, 2005), 305.

8. Wallace, *The Four Immeasurables,* 157–60.

CHAPTER 13

Generosity

1. Chögyam Trungpa, *Shambhala: The Sacred Path of the Warrior,* ed. Carolyn Rose Gimian (Boston: Shambhala Publications, 1998), 47.

CHAPTER 15

Patience

1. Dalai Lama, *Healing Anger: The Power of Patience from a Buddhist Perspective,* trans. Geshe Thupten Jinpa (Ithaca, N.Y.: Snow Lion, 1997), 6–8.

2. Geshe Kelsang Gyatso, *Meaningful to Behold: A Commentary to Shantideva's "Guide to the Bodhisattva's Way of Life"* (London: Tharpa, 1980), 122.

3. Dalai Lama, *Healing Anger,* 9.

4. Ibid. 7.

5. Ibid. 4.

6. Dalai Lama, *A Flash of Lightning in the Dark of Night: A Guide to the Bodhisattva's Way of Life,* trans. Padmakara Translation Group (Boston: Shambhala Publications, 1994), 54–55.

7. Shantideva, *A Guide to the Bodhisattva's Way of Life,* trans. Stephen Batchelor (Dharamsala, India: Library of Tibetan Works and Archives, 1979), 61.

CHAPTER 16

Practices in Patience

1. Thich Nhat Hanh, *Transformations and Healing: Sutra on the Four Establishments of Mindfulness* (Berkeley, Calif.: Parallax Press, 1990), 83–91.

2. Thich Nhat Hanh, "Planting Good Seeds," *Journal of Contemplative Psychotherapy* 7 (1990): 101.

3. Shantideva, *A Guide to the Bodhisattva's Way of Life,* trans. Stephen Batchelor (Dharamsala, India: Library of Tibetan Works and Archives, 1979), 67.

CHAPTER 17
Our Natural Resources

1. Chögyam Trungpa, *The Myth of Freedom and the Way of Meditation,* eds. John Baker and Marvin Casper (Berkeley, Calif.: Shambhala Publications, 1976), 64.

2. Shantideva, *A Guide to the Bodhisattva's Way of Life,* trans. Stephen Batchelor (Dharamsala, India: Library of Tibetan Works and Archives, 1979), 108–14.

3. Ibid. 48–53.

CHAPTER 18
Exertion

1. Shantideva, *A Guide to the Bodhisattva's Way of Life,* trans. Stephen Batchelor (Dharamsala, India: Library of Tibetan Works and Archives, 1979), 86.

2. Ibid. 91.

CHAPTER 19
Meditation

1. Shantideva, *A Guide to the Bodhisattva's Way of Life,* 101.

2. Edward M. Podvoll, "The History of Sanity in Contemplative Psychotherapy," *Naropa Institute Journal of Psychology* 2 (1983), 11–32.

3. Different authors of course present the teachings of the Buddha in a variety of ways. Two among the many excellent sources on the four foundations are Thich Nhat Hanh, *Transformations and Healing: Sutra on the Four Establishments of Mindfulness* (Berkeley, Calif.: Parallax Press, 1990), 83–91, and Mark Epstein, *Going to Pieces without Falling Apart: A Buddhist Perspective on Wholeness: Lessons from Meditation and Psychotherapy* (New York: Broadway Books, 1998), 105–110. I have found Chögyam Trungpa's version of the four foundations of mindfulness, which I am presenting here, to be especially useful in helping clients who are not interested in or ready for sitting meditation practice to cultivate mindfulness. See Chögyam Trungpa, *The Sanity We Are Born With: A Buddhist Approach to Psychology,* ed. Carolyn Rose Gimian (Boston: Shambhala Publications, 2005), 24–42.

4. Karen Kissel Wegela, "Listening Beyond the Words: Working with Exchange," in *Brilliant Sanity: Buddhist Approaches to Psychotherapy*, eds. Francis J. Kaklauskas, Susan Nimanheminda, Louis Hoffman, and MacAndrew Jack (Colorado Springs, Colo.: University of the Rockies Press, 2008), 225–37.
5. Trungpa, *The Sanity We Are Born With*, 32.
6. Ibid. 36.

CHAPTER 20
The Body-Speech-Mind Practice for Working with Exchange
1. Robert Walker, "A Discipline of Inquisitiveness: The 'Body-Speech-Mind' Approach to Contemplative Supervision," in *Brilliant Sanity: Buddhist Approaches to Psychotherapy*, eds. Francis J. Kaklauskas, Susan Nimanheminda, Louis Hoffman, and MacAndrew Jack (Colorado Springs, Colo.: University of the Rockies Press, 2008), 175–94.
2. Bonnie Rabin and Robert Walker, "A Contemplative Approach to Clinical Supervision," *Journal of Contemplative Psychotherapy* 4 (1987): 135–49.

CHAPTER 21
Wisdom
1. Board of editors, "Brilliant Sanity," *Naropa Institute Journal of Psychology* 1 (1980), 1–3.
2. B. Alan Wallace, *The Four Immeasurables: Cultivating a Boundless Heart*, ed. Zara Houshmand, 2nd ed. (Ithaca, N.Y.: Snow Lion, 2004), 152.
3. For more on these approaches, see Edward M. Podvoll, *Recovering Sanity: A Compassionate Approach to Understanding and Treating Psychosis* (Boston: Shambhala Publications, 2003), and Susan Nimanheminda, "Group as Mindfulness Practice," in *Brilliant Sanity: Buddhist Approaches to Psychotherapy*, eds. Francis J. Kaklauskas, Susan Nimanheminda, Louis Hoffman, and MacAndrew Jack (Colorado Springs, Colo.: University of the Rockies Press, 2008), 161–174.

CHAPTER 22
Dedicating the Merit
1. Shantideva, *A Guide to the Bodhisattva's Way of Life*, trans. Stephen Batchelor (Dharamsala, India: Library of Tibetan Works and Archives, 1979), 183.
2. Ibid. 190.
3. Ibid. 193.

bibliography

Aronson, Harvey. *Buddhist Practice on Western Ground: Reconciling Eastern Ideals and Western Psychology.* Boston: Shambhala Publications, 2004.

Beck, Charlotte Joko. *Everyday Zen: Love and Work.* Edited by Steve Smith. San Francisco: HarperSanFrancisco, 1989.

Chödrön, Pema. *No Time to Lose: A Timely Guide to the Way of the Bodhisattva.* Boston: Shambhala Publications, 2005.

———. *The Places That Scare You: A Guide to Fearlessness in Difficult Times.* Boston: Shambhala Publications, 2001.

———. *Start Where You Are: A Guide to Compassionate Living.* Boston: Shambhala Publications, 1994.

Epstein, Mark. *Going to Pieces without Falling Apart: A Buddhist Perspective on Wholeness: Lessons from Meditation and Psychotherapy.* New York: Broadway Books, 1998.

Gyamtso, Khenpo Tsültrim. *Progressive Stages of Meditation on Emptiness.* 2nd ed. Translated by Shenpen Hookham. Oxford, U.K.: Longchen Foundation, 1988.

Gyatso, Geshe Kelsang. *Meaningful to Behold: A Commentary to Shantideva's Guide to the Bodhisattva's Way of Life.* Revised ed. Edited by Jonathan Landaw with Jon Marshall, based on an oral translation by Tenzin P. Phunrabpa. London: Tharpa, 1986.

Gyatso, Tenzin [The Fourteenth Dalai Lama]. *A Flash of Lightning in the Dark of Night: A Guide to the Bodhisattva's Way of Life.* Translated by the Padmakara Translation Group. Boston: Shambhala Publications, 1994.

———. *Healing Anger: The Power of Patience from a Buddhist Perspective.* Translated by Geshe Thupten Jinpa. Ithaca, N.Y.: Snow Lion, 1997.

Hanh, Thich Nhat. *Being Peace.* Edited by Arnold Kotler. Berkeley, Calif.: Parallax Press, 1987.

————. "Planting Good Seeds." *Journal of Contemplative Psychotherapy* 7 (1990): 97–107.

————. *The Practice of Mindfulness in Psychotherapy* 1 and 2. Boulder, Colo.: Sounds True Recordings, 1990. Audiocassettes.

————. *Transformations and Healing: Sutra on the Four Establishments of Mindfulness*. Berkeley, Calif.: Parallax Press, 1990.

Kyabgon, Traleg. *Mind at Ease: Self-Liberation through Mahamudra Meditation*. Boston: Shambhala Publications, 2004.

Nimanheminda, Susan. "Group as Mindfulness Practice." In *Brilliant Sanity: Buddhist Approaches to Psychotherapy*. Edited by Francis J. Kaklauskas, Susan Nimanheminda, Louis Hoffman, and MacAndrew Jack. Colorado Springs, Colo.: University of the Rockies Press, 2008.

Perls, Frederick, Ralph Hefferline, and Paul Goodman. *Gestalt Therapy: Excitement and Growth in the Human Personality*. Gouldsboro, Maine: Gestalt Journal Press, 1994.

Podvoll, Edward M. "The History of Sanity in Contemplative Psychotherapy. *The Naropa Institute Journal of Psychology* 2 (1983): 11–32.

————. *Recovering Sanity: A Compassionate Approach to Understanding and Treating Psychosis*. Boston: Shambhala Publications, 2003.

Rabin, Bonnie and Robert Walker. "A Contemplative Approach to Clinical Supervision," *Journal of Contemplative Psychotherapy* 4 (1987): 135–49.

Rumi. *The Essential Rumi*. Translated by Coleman Barks and John Moyne. San Francisco: HarperSanFrancisco, 1995.

Ryōkan. *One Robe, One Bowl: The Zen Poetry of Ryōkan*. 1st ed.. Translated and introduced by John Stevens. New York: Weatherhill, 1984.

Simmer-Brown, Judith. *Dakini's Warm Breath: The Feminine Principle in Tibetan Buddhism*. Boston: Shambhala Publications, 2002.

Trungpa, Chögyam. *Cutting Through Spiritual Materialism*. Edited by John Baker and Marvin Casper. Boston: Shambhala Publications, 1973.

————. *The Heart of the Buddha*. Edited by Judith L. Lief. Boston: Shambhala Publications, 1991.

————. *The Myth of Freedom and the Way of Meditation*. Edited by John Baker and Marvin Casper. Berkeley, Calif.: Shambhala Publications, 1976.

————. *The Sanity We Are Born With: A Buddhist Approach to Psychology*. Edited by Carolyn Rose Gimian. Boston: Shambhala Publications, 2005.

————. *Shambhala: The Sacred Path of the Warrior*. Edited by Carolyn Rose Gimian. Boston: Shambhala Publications, 1988.

Shantideva. *A Guide to the Bodhisattva's Way of Life*. Translated by Stephen

Batchelor. Dharamsala H.P., India: Library of Tibetan Works & Archives, 1979.

Walker, Robert. "A Discipline of Inquisitiveness: The Body-Speech-Mind Approach to Contemplative Supervision." In *Brilliant Sanity: Buddhist Approaches to Psychotherapy*. Edited by Francis J. Kaklauskas, Susan Nimanheminda, Louis Hoffman, and MacAndrew Jack. Colorado Springs, Colo.: University of the Rockies Press, 2008.

Wallace, B. Alan. *The Four Immeasurables: Cultivating a Boundless Heart*. 2nd ed. Edited by Zara Houshmand. Ithaca, N.Y.: Snow Lion, 2004.

Wegela, Karen Kissel. "Listening Beyond the Words: Working with Exchange." In *Brilliant Sanity: Buddhist Approaches to Psychotherapy*. Edited by Francis J. Kaklauskas, Susan Nimanheminda, Louis Hoffman, and MacAndrew Jack. Colorado Springs, Colo.: University of the Rockies Press, 2008.

Welwood, John. *Toward a Psychology of Awakening: Buddhism, Psychotherapy, and the Path of Personal and Spiritual Transformation*. Boston: Shambhala Publications, 2000.

resources

RECOMMENDED READING

Teachings on Ego, Egolessness, and Emptiness

Chögyam Trungpa, *Cutting Through Spiritual Materialism*, edited by John Baker and Marvin Casper. Berkeley, Calif.: Shambhala Publications, 1973.

Khenpo Tsültrim Gyamtso, *Progressive Stages of Meditation on Emptiness*, 2nd ed., translated by Shenpen Hookham. Oxford, U.K.: Longchen Foundation, 1988.

Khenchen Thrangu, *The Open Door to Emptiness*, translated by Shakya Dorje and edited by Michael L. Lewis. Manila: Tara, 1983.

Teachings on the Four Immeasurables

Pema Chödrön, *The Places That Scare You: A Guide to Fearlessness in Difficult Times*. Boston: Shambhala Publications, 2001.

B. Alan Wallace, *The Four Immeasurables: Cultivating a Boundless Heart*, 2nd ed., edited by Zara Houshmand. Ithaca, N.Y.: Snow Lion, 2004.

Commentaries on Shantideva's Bodhicharyavatara

Pema Chödrön, *No Time to Lose: A Timely Guide to the Way of the Bodhisattva*, edited by Helen Berliner. Boston: Shambhala Publications, 2005.

Geshe Kelsang Gyatso, *Meaningful to Behold: A Commentary to Shantideva's "Guide to the Bodhisattva's Way of Life,"* edited by Jonathan Landaw with Jon Marshall. London: Tharpa, 1985.

Tenzin Gyatso, the Fourteenth Dalai Lama, *A Flash of Lightning in the Dark of Night: A Guide to the Bodhisattva's Way of Life,* translated by the Padmakara Translation Group. Boston: Shambhala Publications, 1994.

To receive information on meditation instruction (as introduced in this book) and related programs, contact one of the following:

Shambhala
Sovereign Place
5121 Sackville Street, Suite 601
Halifax, NS
Canada B3J 1K1
Phone: (902) 425-4275
Website: www.shambhala.org. Information is available on the website about the numerous centers affiliated with Shambhala.

Shambhala Mountain Center
151 Shambhala Way
Red Feather Lakes, CO 80545
Phone: (970) 881-2184
Website: www.shambhalamountain.org

Karmê Chöling
369 Patneaude Lane
Barnet, VT 05821
Phone: (802) 633-2384
Website: www.karmecholing.org

For more information about the MA in contemplative psychotherapy offered by the Contemplative Counseling Psychology Department at Naropa, contact:

Naropa University
2130 Arapahoe Ave.
Boulder, CO 80302
Website: www.naropa.edu
The contemplative psychotherapy program's website: www.naropa.edu /academics/masters/clinical-mental-health-counseling/contemplative -psychotherapy-buddhist-psychology/index.php

index

Printed in the United States
by Baker & Taylor Publisher Services